Communication

A concise introduction to the history of the alphabet, writing, printing, books and libraries.

By

Elmer D. Johnson

Scarecrow Press   New Brunswick, N.J.

1955

Table of Contents

I Early Writing

In the history of man's cultural development, the communication of ideas ranks as one of his most significant achievements. Only when man learned to pass on knowledge that he had accumulated did he become distinguished from the lower animals. Even more significant than the ability to communicate knowledge by means of signs and sounds was the development of a means of preserving knowledge through written records.

This book presents the story of the gradual development of writing, of books and of libraries. The trail from colored pebbles to microcards is long and involved, but is direct and meaningful. Each step leads logically to the next so that the ladder of man's achievements in communicating with his neighbors is clear and substantially continuous.

There are several theories concerning the origin of speech, but there seems to be little doubt that the first medium of communication which primitive man used was the gesture, with or without accompanying vocal sounds. A clenched fist or an upraised arm conveyed a threat, whereas an open palm outstretched could be used to signify friendship or peace. An upraised finger indicated "one;" all fingers outstretched together could have meant "many." With dozens of gestures of arms, hands, fingers, eyes and facial muscles many different ideas could be conveyed without uttering a sound. Add a few gutteral grunts, and most of the necessary communication for primitive society was present. Even today, some primitive Indian tribes depend heavily on gestures in their language. Modern man, despite his well-developed language, still makes use of the gesture, all the way from the nod to indicate agreement to the more elaborate gestures of the public speaker.

Along with the gesture man also developed a spoken

1

language, at first combining the two, then gradually relying more on the voice alone as he became more civilized. Some authorities hold that man's first spoken words were interjections, mere cries of alarm or fear or to attract attention. Next came nouns and pronouns, the names of things and people, followed by verbs, especially the simple verbs of action. Only much later did man add adjectives, beginning with those describing size, number and shape. When he could describe things that were not present, tell of things that had happened in the past, and give vocal form to his imagination he had a true language.

The spoken language, however, was at best only as durable as sound waves and fickle memories. Stories and legends could be told and remembered and re-told to successive generations, but each story teller put his own personality into his version, so that no listener ever heard exactly what his grandfather had heard before him. A history and a literature could be preserved without a written language, but it was a shadowy history and a changeable literature, subject to the whims and imaginations of the tribal story-tellers. In order to preserve history as fact instead of legend, a form of writing was needed, and so the historian today separates the historic eras from the pre-historic at the point where written records began to be made and preserved.

Before writing as we know it began, there were hundreds, perhaps even thousands, of years during which man kept accounts. Man's first attempt at graphic communication was probably a simple sign, such as an arrow pointing the way that a hunting party had taken, or a clan symbol, marking the hunting grounds of one tribe to distinguish it from others. But very early, possibly 10,000 to 15,000 years ago, man began to draw pictures, and to represent in pictorial form what he saw around him. The cave man drew the animals that he knew and hunted. In the caves of southern France and Spain some of these drawings, dated roughly at 10,000 B.C., were very elaborate and realistic, and the artists made use of earth colors and animal fat to embellish their handiwork. More often the primitive drawings were crude and hardly recognizable. There is a question as to whether these drawings were a means of communication or merely an

2

expression of artistic impulse. Was the cave man indicating how many animals he had killed, or simply describing something he had seen? Or were there religious or symbolic meanings attached to these drawings? Sometimes the presence of a weapon or some numerical sign in the drawing indicates clearly that a story is involved and when this is so, we have an early form of hunting chronicle.

Roughly contemporary with these early cave pictures is the colored or marked stone, best known through the "Azilian pebbles," found in the Mas d'Azil area in southern France. These small stones are marked with curious designs and colors, which may be phonetic characters, or numerals, or merely symbols. Various suggestions have been made as to their use and meaning. Some scholars believe that they had some magical or religious value, but conveyed no specific meaning. Others consider them to be something like property markers, family or clan signs, or totems. Still others think they may have been numerical records, indicating the number of animals owned, the number of days passed at some location, or the number of enemies killed. Whatever their meaning, they were an early attempt at writing.

Similar to the Azilian pebbles are many other articles used as mnemonic devices by primitive peoples all over the world. These are not means of communication in the fullest sense of the word, but are merely memory aids, serving to remind the initiated of the main facts of a record or story. Among the best known of these mnemonic devices are the quipus or knotted cord records of the Peruvian Indians. A quipu, by means of different colored cords, of different lengths and knotted in different places, was a means of keeping property records and historical chronicles. The North American Indians had a similar device in their belts of beads or wampum, in which the color, size and position of the shell beads conveyed meaning. In the Middle ages, European peasants often used the clog almanac, a notched stick of wood, to serve as a calendar and remind them of the church festivals and saints' days. Elsewhere, other primitive peoples have made similar use of carved wood or bone, stones or shells, and inscribed or painted hides and

3

bark. Whatever material was used, these mnemonic devices were means of communication, because they did convey meaning to those who understood them.

A step beyond the mnemonic device comes the first form of what might approach true writing. This is the pictograph. The North American Indian used the pictograph as little more than a memory aid. For instance, the "winter count" kept by the Dakota Indians from 1800 to 1870 was simply a series of 71 pictographs inscribed on a buffalo robe. Each picture portrayed the most important event of a winter and it was enough of a reminder to the tribal chronicler to allow him to describe a year's history of the tribe. A step beyond this was the picture story or message. By means of simple drawings, easily recognizable as men, animals, sun, mountains, and other common objects, the Indian could convey a message about a hunting trip, a battle, a love letter, or even a treaty between tribes. At different places and times, American Indians made use of shells, beads, birch bark, tanned hides, woven blankets, painted pottery, and carved sticks as means of recording and conveying information. Yet, despite his versatility in materials, he never quite reached the stage of true writing.

On the other hand, the Egyptian, began with the same type of pictographs and gradually developed them into true writing, capable of recording history, transacting business, or creating a literature. The Egyptian pictograph at first represented what it described and no more. Gradually, however, the pictograph became an ideograph, which conveyed an idea or meaning other than the thing depicted. For example, the picture of an ox might mean "strong," that of the sun could be taken for "bright" or "day," and a man with a crown would of course be "king." We still use ideographs in many forms today, although we hardly ever think of them as such. Many highway signs are ideographs, and so are the signs used in mathematics and music.

The Egyptian advanced from ideographs to the next step in the development of writing; the phonogram, in which the pictographic symbol took on a particular sound, and conveyed that sound-meaning although the pictorial meaning might be different. An example of this would be taking a picture of a bee to represent the verb "be". Next, pictographs with established phonetic values could be put together to form longer words, as if we were to portray "belief" with pictures of a bee and a leaf. The Egyptians made good use of this rebus-like written language, but since they had so many words that sounded alike but had different meanings, they continued to use ideographic signs to distinguish between homophones. For example, if the spoken words for "river" and "palace" were the same, they would add an ideograph for "water" to the "river" phonogram, and possibly a "house" ideograph to that of "castle." Interestingly enough, the modern written Chinese language still contains elements of both ideographs and phonograms.

If the Egyptians had gone one step further the phonograms would have ceased representing syllables and would have retained only their initial sounds, thus becoming a phonetic alphabet. In this case the pictograph for "bee" would represent only the sound "b," and that for the "leaf" would become the "l" sound. (These are not the origins of the letters in question, but are only imaginary examples for purposes of illustration.) The Egyptians never quite achieved a true phonetic alphabet. They had a set of phonetic symbols used only for alphabet sounds, and they sometimes used them for transcribing proper names, but they hesitated to use them alone in ordinary writing, and preferred to accompany them with pictographic elements.

The Egyptian pictographic writing is known as hieroglyphic from the Greek words meaning "sacred carvings." There are examples of hieroglyphic writing that date back more than 4000 years before Christ. The earliest examples found were carved on stone, but very early in Egyptian history a writing material made from the papyrus reed was developed, and thousands of examples of Egyptian papyri have been found, dating over several thousand years. Our word paper come, through the Greek and Latin, from papyrus. The earlier forms of hieroglyphs were pictorial, but by 3000 B.C. a modified form, less recognizable as pictures, was developed. This was the hieratic script, which was more suitable for rapid writing with brush and ink on papyrus. Still a third Egyptian script was the demotic which was used extensively in business and personal writing. Both the hieratic and demotic could be considered as types of shorthand for the original hieroglyphs.

Following the decline of ancient Egypt in the early Christian era, the use of hieroglyphics gave way to Greek and Arabic scripts, and for some fifteen hundred years no one was able to translate the examples found. Finally, in the early nineteenth century, the Rosetta stone, a curiously inscribed plaque, was taken to France from Egypt by Napoleon's soldiers. This stone carried three inscriptions, one in Greek, one in hieroglyphics, and one in demotic, all apparently giving the same message. The Greek could be read, but this did not immediately result in deciphering the Egyptian. Several scholars studied the stone over a period of years and, finally, Jean François Champollion discovered the key to the hieroglyphics. Champollion guessed that certain enclosed groups of hieroglyphic characters represented proper names, and, knowing these names from the ac- companying Greek text, he was able to begin assigning values to the hundreds of separate Egyptian characters. It was a long task, and other scholars, English, French and German, contributed to it, but Champollion is usual- ly given credit for first reading Egyptian hieroglyphics. Through our knowledge of the Egyptian script, a vast amount of knowledge concerning the life and history of the Nile valley peoples has been made available to modern scholars.

Over in the Mesopotamian valley, in what is today Iraq, another civilization grew up simultaneously with that of ancient Egypt. This was the Sumerian-Babylon- ian-Assyrian civilization, which existed from before 3000 B.C. to about 500 B.C. These peoples also de- veloped a system of writing based on pictographs, but showing little similarity to that of the Egyptians. The Sumerians and their successors had little stone and no papyrus, so they turned to clay tablets for their writing materials. A sharp pointed stylus of wood or metal was used to make impressions in soft clay, and the clay was allowed to harden, or it was baked into bricks if a permanent record was desired. The stylus-

6

on-clay method of writing did not lend itself to elaborate pictographs, and so the Sumerian writing assumed
the form of stylized diagrams made by short wedge-
shaped strokes in the clay. This writing, known as
cuneiform (Latin for wedge-shaped), was further simplified by the Babylonians and Assyrians until in its latest
known form there is little resemblance between the cuneiform character and the original pictograph from
which it developed. Like the Egyptian, the cuneiform
writing developed through the ideograph to the phonetic
syllable, and never developed to the phonetic alphabet,
although the number of phonetic symbols was reduced
to about 400. After the destruction of Babylon by the
Persians in the seventh century B.C., the conquerors
took some thirty-six of the cuneiform symbols and used
them as a strictly phonetic alphabet.

The account of the deciphering and translating of cuneiform is almost as romantic as that of the Rosetta
stone. Examples of the clay tablets had been known
for centuries, and many scholars had attempted to de-
cipher them. Sir Henry Rawlinson was sent to Persia
early in the nineteenth century to drill the army of the
Shah. In his spare time he toured the ruins of ancient
civilizations in and around Persia. On one of these
expeditions he came upon an inscription chiseled into
the bare rock face of a high cliff. This inscription,
known as the Rock of Behistun, was in three languages,
Babylonian, Mede or Scythian, and Old Persian. The
Persian could be read, and after many years of study,
Rawlinson finally deciphered the other two scripts. The
Babylonian was most important, because it opened up
a vast amount of knowledge that had been imprisoned
in the clay tablets and cuneiform inscriptions available
in the Mesopotamian area. The deciphering of the
Behistun inscription came within ten years of Champollion's similar achievement with the Rosetta stone.

Other ancient scripts have not yet been deciphered.
These include the pictographic writing of the Hittites,
another Semitic people of Asia Minor who lived and
flourished about 1500 B.C., and a form of writing known
to have been used in the ancient, pre-Hellenic civilization of the island of Crete. This latter writing bears
some resemblance to a phonetic alphabet, and some

authorities think it may have been the ancestor of the Phoenician alphabet, but we have no proof of this. In the ruins of the Mayan civilization of Central America a highly developed hieroglyphic writing has been discovered. Some of the numbers and dates in this script have been deciphered, but for the most part it remains unread. Stone inscriptions found on Easter Island, and other islands in the Pacific also defy translation. These and other undeciphered scripts await another Rawlinson or Champollion to discover their keys, but in most cases there are so few examples of a particular type of writing remaining, that it is doubtful that an accurate reading will ever be achieved.

Apparently every people, wherever they might be, began their writing with pictographs. Some of them advanced further to phonetic alphabets, while others, like the Egyptians, Babylonians and Chinese failed to get past the syllabary stage, although otherwise they developed highly civilized societies. European civilization owes its phonetic alphabet to the Phoenicians. These sea-faring, trading people lived along the eastern end of the Mediterranean, on the coasts of what is now Palestine and Syria. Being merchants, they had contacts with many neighbors, both near and far, including the Egyptians, Hebrews, Cretans, Hittites, and Babylonians. In one or more respects, each of these peoples was more advanced than the Phoenicians. Yet it was the Phoenicians who first made general use of an easily learned, simply written alphabet. Perhaps it was because they needed such a script for their business transactions, and because the Egyptian demotic, which they could have used, did not adapt itself readily to the Phoenician language. The origin of the Phoenician alphabet is uncertain, but it is known that they were using a twenty-two letter, all consonant alphabet by about 900 B.C. What we know about the cultural history of the Phoenicians indicates that they adapted it from some neighboring civilization. Some believe it came from the demotic, others from early Cretan script, or the Hittite or Babylonian cuneiform. One source traces the Phoenician alphabet to a very early form of writing from India. Probably the best theory is that it was developed from an early semi-alphabet that was in use by a Semitic people on the Sinai peninsula about 1500 B.C. This

Sinaitic script bears closer resemblance to the early
Phoenician letters than any of the other suggested
sources. Whatever the source of the alphabet, the
Phoenicians popularized it in the Mediterranean world
and passed it on to the Greeks.

The Greeks took the phonetic alphabet, adapted it to
their own language, and used it to create a great literature. The Phoenicians had used an alphabet consisting entirely of consonants, but the Greeks used some
of the Phoenician letters as vowels, added others to
represent phonetic values that were present in the
Greek language but not in the Phoenician, and began
the custom of writing from left to right. In addition,
the Greeks used different forms for making the same
letters, gradually developing them into something like
our capital and lower case letters, although their
purpose was not the same. Their capitals were used
generally for inscriptions on stone or wood, and their
small letters for ordinary writing. From Greece, the
alphabet passed to Rome. Minor changes have been
made, including additions of letters in some languages,
such as the "W" in English, but for the most part the
alphabet of the classic Roman period is the same as
ours today.

The alphabet as we know it in the English language
is much the same as that used by the French, Spanish,
Portuguese, Italians, Dutch, Scandinavians, and, in Gothic
form, the Germans. Some modern eastern European
countries also use the Latin alphabet, while others use
an alphabet developed from old Cyrillic, which grew out
of the ancient Greek in a different form from the Latin.
The Arabic and Hebrew alphabets, along with other Near
Eastern and Southeast Asian alphabets, developed from
the Phoenician or from a common ancestor.

Writing Materials

In most ancient scripts, the form of the characters
or letters often varied with the material on which the
writing was done. Thus the Egyptian hieratic, the Babylonian cuneiform, and the Latin capitals were developed
to accomodate the materials on which they were most
effectively used, papyrus, clay, and stone, respectively.
The earliest writing materials were probably bone or

wood surfaces, marked with charred sticks or sharp stones, but these materials do not lend themselves to preservation, so few examples of such writing are known. Later the writing was done on tanned or treated hides, or on early forms of textiles, but these, too, did not keep very well. But when man began carving on stone, as the Egyptians often did, a very permanent record resulted. Such carving was difficult and was used only for the most important writings.

For a plentiful, cheaper writing material, the E-gyptians turned to the wild papyrus reeds which grew profusely along the Nile. While the papyrus was still young and green it was cut, split, and the pithy inside core was removed and dried. This fibrous core was then pressed flat, laid in strips, and covered by an-other layer of strips at right angles. A resinous glue was then applied, and the whole was again pressed and dried. The result was a thin sheet of rather porous but durable writing material. The surface of the pa-pyrus was polished with a piece of ivory, bone, or shell. Papyrus sheets were made usually in sizes of about five by eleven inches; when larger sizes were needed, sheets were pasted together, and rolls more than a hundred feet long have been found. The ink used for writing on papyrus was made from lampblack, or powdered charcoal, mixed with a gum solution and thinned with water. Red inks were made with a gum base colored by oxide of iron, and blue ink with the same base colored with powdered lapis lazuli. The inks were put on paper with reed pens, made from the dried reeds sharpened to a point, and with the point then chewed or blunted into a soft brush tip.

The papyrus reed was grown mostly in the fertile Nile valley, and hence most of the papyrus was made there. As the demand grew it was exported to the other Mediterranean countries. Egypt had something of a monopoly on the production of papyrus, and its manu-facture became an important industry. Papyrus was made in various qualities, and different names were ap-plied to the various types, according to thickness, finish and quality. Trade in papyrus was an important business, and the Phoenicians considered papyrus one of their most important items of commerce. It continued to be used until the eleventh century, A.D., and must have served as a writing material for well over 4000 years.

Shortage of papyrus in Pergamum, a Greek state in Asia Minor resulted in use of tanned hides for writing materials. This led to the development of parchment (a word derived from pergamena, the Latin form of Pergamum) which is finely tanned sheepskin. Tanned hides had been used as writing materials in prehistoric times, but the preparation of parchment, which is a split, tanned and bleached hide, apparently originated in Asia Minor about the fifth century B.C. Parchment and its close relative, vellum (made from calf skin), came into wide use in the next few centuries and gradually replaced papyrus, particularly in the Roman world, and for important writings. In ordinary use, the terms parchment and vellum are sometimes used inter-changeably. These materials were used extensively to the nineteenth century, and are still used for very important documents. The best grades of parchment had an excellent writing surface which took not only inks, but colored oils as well, and thus could be elaborately lettered and decorated. The use of vellum and parchment brought a change in the writing implement also. The brush-tipped reed gave way to the sharpened, split-point reed, and then to the split-feather quill. The Romans in particular made good use of the quill, and our word "pen" comes from the Latin word for "feather." The feather quill was used as a writing implement for at least 2000 years, and the metal pen-point which we use today is a faithful copy of it.

From Roll to Book

The roll form of the papyrus "book" continued in use long after the development of parchment. The Romans made good use of another writing material, the waxed tablet. A thin wooden board, or a sheet of metal or ivory, was covered with a thin layer of wax. A metal stylus was employed for writing on the wax, and a smooth, blunt instrument could be used to "erase" the writing for corrections, or to leave the surface of the wax completely free of marks and ready to be used again. This "tabula" (from which we get our word tablet had the advantage of being usable again and again,

11

whereas papyrus and parchment could be used only once, or at best erased with difficulty. The tabula was widely used by Roman school children, and it was also used in business houses for temporary records and for computing sums. Letters could be sent on these waxed tablets, and when this was done the tabula usually took the form of a diptych, two boards hinged together at one side, with the waxed surfaces on the inside, and thus protected. In general form and appearance, the diptych suggested the modern book, although it had two pages only.

Roughly contemporary with the tabula there arose another book form, the codex, which may have been developed from, or suggested by, the diptych. The codex was made by folding a long strip of parchment or papyrus that had originally been rolled, into accordion-like pleats. For many years, the codex remained simply folded, but eventually it became common to sew the folds along one side, making a "book" of doubled leaves. Some Chinese and Japanese books are still made in this form. The codex with the doubled leaves was uneconomical because it wasted one side of each sheet. So another form of codex was made by folding a sheet double the size of the page wanted. This made a "book" of four pages, or by folding several sheets together, a quire of eight, twelve, sixteen or more pages could be prepared. Then these were sewn along the fold, and, if necessary, several quires could be sewn together to form a thicker book. When "backs" of wood or leather were added, the form of the codex had reached substantially that of the modern book. Despite the coming of the codex, which was in general use by the fourth century, A.D., the roll retained its popularity until the beginning of printing.

BIBLIOGRAPHY

Allen, Agnes: The story of the book. London, 1952. See pp. 1-31.

American Council on Education: The story of writing. Washington, 1931. 64 p.

Baikie, James: Egyptian papyri and papyrus hunting. London, 1925. 324 p.

Brinton, Daniel G.: A primer of Mayan hieroglyphs. Boston, 1895. 152 p.

Budge, Ernest A.W.: The Rosetta stone in the British Museum. London, 1929. 325 p.

Bushnell, G.H.: From papyrus to print. London, 1947. (See pp. 9-13 for a good description of the making of papyrus.)

Chiera, Edward: They wrote on clay: The Babylonian tablets speak today. Chicago, 1938. 235 p.

Davenport, Cyril: The book. 257 p. New York, 1930. (See pp. 1-25.)

Denman, Frank: The shaping of our alphabet. New York, 1955. 232 p.

Diringer, D.: The alphabet, a key to the history of mankind. New York, 1951. 607 p.

Driver, Godfrey R.: Semitic writing from pictograph to alphabet. Oxford, 1948. 222 p.

Gelb, I.J.: A study of writing. Chicago, 1952. 296 p.

Hamilton, Frederick W.: Books before typography; a primer of information about the invention of the alphabet. Chicago, 1918. 47 p.

Hogben, Lancelot: From cave painting to comic strip; a kaleidoscope of human communication. New York, 1949. 286 p.

Hunter, Dard: Papermaking: the history and technique of an ancient craft. 611 p. New York, 1947. (See pp. 3-48.)

McMurtrie, Douglas C.: The book: the story of printing and bookmaking. New York, 1943. 676 p. (See pp. 1-39.)

Mallory, Garrick: Picture writing of the North American Indians. Washington, 1888. 807 p. (10th Annual Report of the Bureau of American Ethnology).

Marshak, Ilia J.: Black on white, the story of books. Philadelphia, 1932. 135 p.

Mason, William: A history of the art of writing. New York, 1928. 502 p.

Ogg, Oscar: An alphabet source book. New York, 1940. 199 p.

Petrie, William M.F.: The formation of the alphabet. London, 1912. 20 p.

Pumphrey, R.J.: The origin of language. Liverpool, University Press, 1951. 39 p.

Roberts, Ernest S.: An introduction to Greek epigraphy. Cambridge, England, 1905. 2 vols.

Sandys, John E.: Latin epigraphy. Cambridge, England, 1919. 324 p.

Smith, A. M.: Printing and writing materials, their evolution. Philadelphia, 1901. 236 p.

Sprengling, Martin: The alphabet; its rise and development from the Sinai inscriptions. Chicago, 1931. 71 p.

Taylor, Isaac: The history of the alphabet. New York, 1899. 2 v.

Thompson, Tommy: The ABC of our alphabet. New York, 1942. 64 p.

Ullman, Berthold L,: Ancient writing and its influence. New York, 1932. 234 p.

Van Hoesen, Henry B.: Bibliography. New York, 1928. 519 p. (See pp. 259-313.)

Waddell, Lawrence A.: The Aryan origin of the alphabet. London, 1927. 80 p.

"Alphabet," Encyclopedia Britannica, 11th ed., (1916), I, 723-732; 14th ed., (1948), I, 677-685.

Conder, C.R.: "Origin of alphabets", Edinburgh Review, CLXXII, (1890), 112-140.

Guppy, Henry: "Human records, a survey of their history from the beginnings," John Rylands Library Bulletin, XXVII, (1942), 182-222.

Hackh, I.W.D.: "History of the alphabet," Scientific Monthly, XXV, (1927), 97-118.

Praetorius, Franz: "The origin of the Canaanite alphabet," Annual Report of the Smithsonian Institution, 1907, 595-604.

Swanton, John R.: "The quipu and Peruvian civilization," Bureau of American Ethnology, Anthropological Papers, XXVI, 587-596.

Williams, Henry S.: "The history of the alphabet," Harpers Monthly, CVIII, (1904), 534-540.

"Writing," Encyclopedia Britannica, 11th ed., (1916), XXVIII, 847-853.

II Ancient Libraries

After civilized man began to make and keep written
records, the formation of libraries was a logical development. The earliest form of library was what we
would now consider an archive, for it was really a
compilation of government or religious documents.
Ancient Egypt, one of the earliest areas to develop
writing, produced some of the earliest libraries of
which we have any record. These libraries were composed of papyrus rolls, and they were generally of two
kinds: government archives or private libraries.

Government archives contained mainly official
records and chronologies, accounting for the events in
the reigns of various kings, or the accomplishments of
officials in collecting taxes or building monuments.
Some records of court cases and chronicles of military
expeditions have been preserved. The temple libraries
included church records, religious writings, and the
lives of the various Egyptian gods.

A few of the wealthier Egyptian nobles and business
men maintained private libraries, and since examples
of these books were buried with their owners in their
tombs, we know more about them than we know about the
official archives. They were of papyrus, tightly rolled
and kept in labelled pottery jars in orderly rows on
shelves. The contents of the private libraries were
often similar to those of the government, including
business and family records and correspondence, but
some included more exciting reading in the form of
travel stories, tales of wars and adventures, and books
of magic. There were often a few rolls concerned with
science, mathematics or medicine, usually connected
with magic, and probably in all Egyptian libraries there
were copies of the most famous of all Egyptian books,
the "Book of the Dead." This was a book of religious
ritual designed to guide the souls of the dead through

the underworld to the hall of judgment, where one's permanent position in the next world was decided. The production of copies of the "Book of the Dead" was a profitable business, and the length and elaborateness of each copy varied with the wealth and importance of the person buying it. A copy now preserved in the British Museum is seventy-eight feet long and fifteen inches wide, and contains many colorful illustrations.

The librarian of the ancient Egyptian library was probably the court or temple scribe, who helped to write and to preserve the papyrus rolls. Wealthy nobles hired scribes to care for their books, or had slaves trained as librarians. The papyrus rolls were kept in clay jars or metal cylinders, with a few key words of the title on the side or end. Little is known of the method of arrangement of the rolls, but it was probably by title. The list of the contents of one such library can still be read on the walls of the temple at Edfu.

Since Babylonia and Assyria made their books of baked clay, literally thousands of them have been preserved. Evidences of many government, religious and private libraries have been found in the ruins of the Mesopotamian cities. Considering that the Egyptian collections were largely archives, the Assyrians may be said to have produced the first real library. We know that they achieved very large collections of tablets, systematically gathered and arranged, and including all types of literature. One of the Assyrian kings, Assurbanipal (668-626 B.C.), is noted for his library. Under his direction there was gathered at Nineveh, his capital, a library of many thousands of clay tablets, and a score or more copyists and clerks arranged and preserved them under the direction of a royal librarian. The tablets were arranged roughly by subject or type, lettered on the outside according to their contents, and placed on rows of narrow shelves. Some of the more important tablets were encased in another clay shell, which had to be broken before its contents could be read. A catalog or description of the contents was painted or carved on the door of each room or cubicle of the library. In this royal library there were government documents, historical chronologies, official letters,

religious texts, and miscellaneous works in the fields of
science and law. Unfortunately the Assyrian civilization
was virtually destroyed in wars during the sixth and
seventh centuries, B.C., and the magnificent library was
reduced to a pile of rubble. So indestructible were the
baked brick tablets, however, that about 22,000 of them
were recovered from the ruins twenty-five centuries
later. Most of these are preserved in the British Museum. Other collections of clay tablets have been found
in ruins of various Mesopotamian cities, indicating that
there were probably other public or private libraries
dating back as far as 3000 B.C.

Although Greece's great age of literature was in the
fifth and fourth centuries, B.C., when Plato and
Aristotle flourished, we know relatively little of Greek
libraries of that era. Certainly those scholars had
fairly large private libraries of their own, and the history of Aristotle's private library is known for several
centuries after his death. Book copiers and book
sellers were active in Greece and literature in the form
of papyrus rolls was plentiful for those who could afford
it. By the third century, B.C., there were probably
governmental or royal libraries in Athens and other
Greek mainland cities, since we know that there were
libraries in the Greek colonies, but facts about them
are few.

Though we have little information about libraries in
Greece itself, we have fairly substantial evidence of
important libraries in the outposts of Greek civilization.
Under Philip and Alexander, Greek political and cultural
power spread from Sicily to the Black Sea, and from
the Balkans far up the Egyptian Nile. We know of a
library supported by the government at the Greek colony
of Heracleia, on the Black Sea. Other great libraries
were reported to have existed at Syracuse in Sicily.
Also, there was the one at Pergamum. According to
the Greek biographer, Plutarch, the library at Pergamum
contained over 200,000 rolls and was housed in a beautiful building. Antony is supposed to have taken the
Pergamum library as spoils of war and presented it to
Cleopatra.

The greatest library stemming from Greek cultural

domination grew up at Alexandria, in Egypt, under the Greek-Egyptian rulers, Ptolemy I and II. In the third century, B.C., a few years after its founding, the Alexandrian library was reported to contain over a half million rolls. It was housed in its own building, across from the royal palace, and staffed by forty or more scholar-librarians. Manuscripts were acquired from all the known world, in Egyptian, Greek, Latin, Hebrew and other languages. In most cases translations were made into Greek, and different copies of individual works were compared and edited in order to achieve the most authentic texts. A pre-Christian version of the Hebrew Old Testament (the Septuagint) is thought to have been compiled here by seventy scholars under orders from Ptolemy I in 270 B.C.

Several outstanding names in Greek literature have been connected with the Alexandrian library. One of the early head librarians was the poet Callimachus, and others include Eratosthenes, astronomer and mathematician, and Aristophanes of Byzantium, also a noted scholar. Callimachus was a bibliographer as well as a poet; he made a catalog of the library, by author and title, and divided it into major subject or form groups such as epic poetry, dramatic poetry, laws, philosophy, history and oratory. Callimachus' Pinakes, as his catalog or bibliography was called, was in reality something of a literary encyclopedia. It was said to have been contained in 120 rolls and to have included, besides bibliographic information, short excerpts from the works themselves. One author gives the sub-title of the Pinakes as "Tables of all those who were eminent in any kind of literature and of their writings". Though this work has not been preserved, excerpts from it appear in the books of later authors.

The fate of the Alexandrian Library is almost as uncertain as the names of its later librarians. At its height it attracted scholars from all over the Mediterranean world. After the Romans extended their conquests to Egypt, rebelling Egyptians burned much of the city, including a major part of the Alexandrian Library. Some of it survived and major additions were made to it from time to time. Some three centuries later, in 272 A.D., another Roman conqueror, Aurelian,

18

destroyed Alexandria and with it the famous library.
Some writers insist that at least a part of it survived
four centuries more, only to be completely destroyed at
the orders of the Caliph Omar following the Moslem
conquest of Egypt in 642 A.D. Whatever its fate, it
was the greatest library of the ancient world, and its
loss is one of the tragedies of history.

Greek cities also developed notable libraries during
the same period. Athens probably had several important book collections, including that in the Ptolema-
eum, or gymnasium of Ptolemy. Aristides, the rheto-
rician, writing in the second century, said that Athens
had the finest libraries in the world. The university of
Rhodes was built around a library, and the city of
Rhodes was noted as being, next to Athens, the best
book market in the Greek world. The trade center of
Corinth had a library, as did also the Greek cities of
Smyrna and Ephesus in Asia Minor. Most of these
libraries fell into Roman hands, either to be destroyed,
or to be carried off to Rome.

The Romans took from the countries they conquered
many cultural developments. Not only did they acquire
the idea of libraries, but the books themselves were
taken from Greece, Asia Minor and Egypt to fill the
shelves of the Roman libraries. In many cases, educated citizens of the conquered countries, particularly
Greeks, were brought as slaves to become the teachers,
scribes, and librarians of Rome. Roman culture was
heavily indebted to Greece and Egypt, but in libraries,
as in law, the Romans improved on their predecessors.

In the second century, B.C., Paulus, who had defeated
the Macedonians, brought home a Greek library as his
personal spoils of war, and in the next century, Sulla
and Lucullus did likewise. Lucullus went on from his
conquests to become an ardent collector of books, and
threw open his library to all scholars who came to use
it. A few years later, Julius Caesar drew up plans for
a public library in Rome, and he commissioned Varro
to collect books for it. Caesar's library never materi-
alized, but it may have provided the plan for the library
founded by Caius Asinius Pollio during the reign of
Augustus, which is usually mentioned as the first public

library in Rome. Augustus later founded two public libraries, each divided into two divisions, one for Greek and one for Latin books. Following Augustus, most of the later emperors founded libraries, either in Rome, or in other cities, so that by the middle of the fourth century, A.D., there were no less than twenty-nine public libraries in Rome alone. The Ulpian Library in the Forum of Trajan, built early in the second century, A.D., was probably typical of these imperial libraries. The center of the Forum was a colonnaded court, with the Greek library on one side and the Latin library on the other. Each library was about 60 feet long by 45 feet wide, with alcoves or small reading-rooms at each end. Busts of the important Greek and Latin authors stood guard over their respective works. Some of these public libraries were reported to have 100,000 or more volumes.

The public libraries in Rome approached our modern conception of public libraries in that they were not only publicly owned, but they were freely used by any citizen who could read, and it was not uncommon to see both nobleman and slave using them at the same time. In organization, the Roman libraries were apparently patterned after those of Greece and Egypt, with the rolls arranged according to subject or title on shelves or in bins. The average book was rolled on a wooden core and preserved in a leather wrapper, or perhaps in an earthen jar, but the more valuable and more elaborate works were sometimes wrapped around an ivory center and preserved in bronze cylinders. In the third century, A.D., Roman libraries began to contain folded or book-form codices. Except in rare cases, books had to be used in the library or in adjacent reading rooms.

There were several grades of library workers in the Roman libraries, including possibly at times an imperial library administrator who supervised all the public libraries in Rome. Each library had its own administrator or procurator who apparently concerned himself with acquisition and administrative duties. The more direct work with the books was done by "bibliotheca," who cared for them and kept them in order. There were several types of bibliotheca, indicating that there were library specialists even in ancient Rome. Also

connected with the library was the "librarius," who
seems to have been a transcriber or copyist who dupl-
cated borrowed works, or made additional copies of
those already in the library. It is interesting to note
that some of these copyists were women, and that in
many cases slaves filled all of the library positions be-
low that of the procurator.

Many of the private libraries were almost as large
and elaborate as the public libraries. Cicero had a
large book collection of his own, and the physician,
Sammonicus, of the third century, A.D., was reported
to have built up a library of over 60,000 volumes. In
the ruins of Herculaneum, a city destroyed in the e-
ruption of Mount Vesuvius in 79 A.D., there has been
found the remains of a large private library. This collection of about 1700 rolls was found in a room about
twelve feet square with the walls lined with book cases
all the way to the ceiling. The rolls were charred and
in very bad condition but careful treatment has made
many of them readable. Apparently this collector
specialized in the works of the Epicurean philosophers,
and there is some evidence that the owner was the
philosopher Philodemus. The collecting of books and
the building of private libraries became such a fad a-
mong the wealthy noblemen and merchants of Rome
that Seneca is supposed to have said, "Nowadays a
library is considered a necessary ornament with which
to adorn a house, along with hot and cold baths." The
larger private libraries also had their librarians, usually slaves, to keep them in order and to copy works
from other libraries.

Closely connected with libraries, then as always, was
the book manufacturer and the book seller. In prosper-
ous times the demand for copies of books was so great
the the wholesale publishing of certain works was
profitable. An enterprising business man would hire a
number of scribes, or perhaps purchase slaves who
could write a good hand, and set them to copying the
book in demand. One would read from the text, while
ten or twelve writers would copy. There were a
number of such book makers in Rome, some of whom
were renowned for the quality of their work. Also
there were bookseller's shops that specialized in these

copies. Adjoining the book stores were posts on which lists of books for sale were posted. On market days the booksellers sometimes used public criers, who stood before the shop and proclaimed the volumes for sale. Another interesting custom connected with the Roman book shop was its recital room, where would-be authors could read or recite their works to anyone who cared to listen. If a listener was captivated enough by the recital to purchase a copy, a scribe was set to work to produce it.

The great era of Roman libraries lasted five hundred years, and then, like so many other book collections of the classic period, those of Rome were destroyed. Most of the Roman libraries were ransacked in the barbarian attacks on the city in the fifth century, A.D., and much of our knowledge about them comes from the volcano-buried cities of Pompeii and Herculaneum. Some of the religious literature was preserved in monasteries in Italy during the period after the fall of Rome, but most of the secular books that survived were among those transferred to Constantinople, the capital of the Eastern Roman Empire. There these literary treasures contributed to the greatness of the Byzantine civilization for a thousand years. Most of the classic Greek and Roman literature that we have today was preserved either in the libraries of Constantinople or in the monasteries of Greece and Asia Minor.

The libraries of Constantinople were notable. Emperor Constantine I, who founded Constantinople, began the royal library in the early fourth century with 6,000 volumes. Three centuries later it contained over 100,000 volumes, and was probably the greatest library in the world. But the Byzantine libraries--and there were others besides the royal library--were rivaled by new ones springing up in the Moslem world in the seventh and eighth centuries. The followers of Mohammed esteemed the book second only to the sword, and although for the majority of the people there was only one book, the Koran, there were many scholars who translated and preserved the Greek and Roman literature. As early as 689 a library and archival collection was founded at Damascus, then the headquarters of the newly created Moslem faith. In the next century, after Baghdad became the seat of the most important Moslem Caliph, a large public library was opened there and its use was free to all who could read. Manuscripts were gathered from all over the known world and scholars came from hundreds of miles. Other Moslem cities, from Bokhara, in Central Asia, to Cordoba, in Spain, also had large libraries during this period. In the tenth century, in Cairo, a Caliph's library was reported to contain over a million rolls. It was cataloged in forty-four rolls. This library had a large staff paid from the income from lands owned by the library.

The ancient library was a product of its civilization. It appeared whenever a people had reached the point where they had writing materials, a written language, and records to preserve. It progressed in size, complexity and elaborateness as civilization itself advanced. When a civilization was overthrown by a more primitive people, books and libraries disappeared, and ignorance returned. If our study of ancient libraries teaches us nothing else, it shows us that books and libraries always accompany any advanced culture.

Bibliography

Boyd, Clarence E.: Public libraries and literary culture in ancient Rome. Chicago, 1915. 69 p.

Brassington, William S.: A history of the art of bookbinding with some account of the books of the ancients. London, 1894. 270 p.

Budge, Ernest A.W.: The literature of the ancient Egyptians. London, 1914. 272 p.

Bushnell, G.H.: The world's earliest libraries. London 1931. 58 p.

Chiera, Edward   They wrote on clay: the Babylonian tablets speak today. Chicago, 1938. 235 p.

Clark, J.W.: The care of books; an essay on the development of libraries and their fittings. Cambridge, England, 1902. 352 p.

Holliday, Carl: The dawn of literature. New York, 1931. 367 p.

Hessel, Alfred: A history of libraries. New Brunswick, 1955. 198 p.

Jast, Louis S.: The library and the community. London, 1939, 204 p. (See pp. 13-24 on "Oldest Libraries".)

Kenyon, Frederic G.: Ancient books and modern discoveries. Chicago, 1927. 83 p.

------ Books and readers in ancient Greece and Rome. Oxford, 1932. 136 p.

Lanciani, Rodolfo: Ancient Rome in the light of recent discoveries. Boston, 1900. 329 p. (See pp. 178-205 on "The public libraries of ancient and medieval Rome".)

Maspero, Gaston: Life in ancient Egypt and Assyria. New York, 1912. 376 p. (See pp. 287-302 on "Assurbanipal's Library".)

Middleton, J.H.: Illuminated manuscripts in classical and medieval times. Cambridge, England, 1892. 270 p.

Myer, Isaac: The oldest books in the world. New York, 1900. 502 p.

Nichols, Charles L.: The library of Rameses the Great. Boston, 1909. 43 p.

Parsons, Edward A.: The Alexandrian library. New York, 1952. 468 p.

Pinner, H.L.: The world of books in classical antiquity. Leiden, Netherlands, 1948. 64 p.

Putnam, George H.: Authors and their public in ancient times. New York, 1894. 326 p.

Richardson, Ernest C.: Beginnings of libraries. Princeton, 1914. 176 p.

------ Biblical libraries. Princeton, 1914. 252 p.

------ Some old Egyptian libraries. New York, 1911 93 p.

Thompson, James W.: Ancient libraries. Chicago, 1939. 120 p.

Van Hook, La Rue: Greek life and thought. New York, 1923. 329 p. (See pp. 114-121 on "Greek Libraries".)

Anon.: "The library of the Assyrian King, Sardanapolus," Scientific American, CII, (1910), 126.

Miller, Walter: "Hadrian's library and Gymnasium," Art and Archeology, XXXIII, (January, 1932), 89-91.

Rau, R.V.: "Did Omar destroy the Alexandrian Library?" Nineteenth Century, XXXVI, (1894), 555-571.

Reichman, Felix: "The book trade at the time of the Roman Empire", Library Quarterly, VIII, (January, 1938), 40-76.

Root, Robert K.: "Publication before printing," Publications of the Modern Language Association, XXVIII, (1913), 417-431.

Wyss, Wilhelm V.: "The libraries of antiquity," Living Age, CCCXVI, (Jan. 27, 1923), 217-249.

III Books and Libraries in the Middle Ages

After the fall of Rome in 476 A.D., Europe entered almost a thousand years of the Dark Ages. The cultural progress that Rome had made largely disappeared as wave after wave of barbarians swept out of central and northern Europe and overran the Roman world. The libraries of Rome and the other civilized centers of western Europe were ransacked and burned, and only a few copies survived from the many thousands of books that had made Rome a city of learning. Not until the modern era would there again be libraries in Europe that could compare with those of the classical period, and not until the Renaissance would there be very much added to the secular literature that Greece and Rome had left to posterity. Even before 476, papyrus had given away to vellum and parchment as writing materials, and the roll had been replaced by the codex, which became the predominant book-form of the Middle Ages. From then until the coming of printing, there was no change in the laborious process of writing and binding books by hand, although it must be admitted that this hand-making of books became an art. In illustrating, or illuminating, and in bindings, the best medieval manuscript books equal or surpass anything printed today.

In the midst of the dark ages, there were several forces at work, though not always together, to preserve something of the culture of Rome and Greece, and to keep alive the learning of that advanced age. The institution usually credited with preserving books and learning during the Middle Ages is the monastery, and undoubtedly it did play a major role. Private book collectors also took part in preserving the classics, especially the non-religious ones. These private book collectors were wealthy merchants or noblemen, particularly of Venice, Genoa, Marseilles and the other Mediterranean cities. Many of them collected manuscripts

26

for show and prestige; but whatever their motives, they did acquire, preserve, and copy many notable works. After the eleventh century, the medieval university took its place as an active participant in collecting, editing and copying the earlier authors. The Moslem world, from Persia to Spain, did its share to preserve the writings of the Greeks and Romans, as did also the Byzantine civilization around Constantinople. Occasional enlightened rulers, the Charlemagnes and Alfreds, whose reigns stand out like beacons in an otherwise gloomy era, also aided in the preservation of culture.

The monastery had its beginnings during the Roman era, but most of the more outstanding ones in Europe proper date from a later period. St. Benedict founded Monte Cassino in Italy in 529, and a famous library was associated with this monastery almost from the beginning. Cassiodorus, a noble who had served with the ruler, Theodoric the Goth, retired from his office in 543 to live as a monk on his estate in Callabria, in southern Italy. He began two monasteries, one of which, at Viviers, he endowed with his own private library. Among his other accomplishments were the writing of a History of the Goths, and a handbook of monastery rules and regulations, which included a section on use of the monastery library. In France there were early important monastic libraries at Cluny, Fleury and Corbie. The library of the monastery at Cluny, in northern France, founded in 910, had more than five hundred volumes, which was large for a monastery collection. Even before the founding of Cluny there were monasteries in all of northern Europe, from Ireland to Poland, and most of them were rather faithful copies of earlier ones in Italy and Greece. Ireland, by the seventh century, had monasteries that were renowned for the quantity and quality of their books, and from Ireland something of a renaissance spread to England, where important churches and monasteries were established at Canterbury, York, Whitby and Durham, and a few other spots. Monks from these monasteries made the long and arduous trip to Rome, sometimes several times during their lives, to obtain copies of precious religious works for their own and other English libraries.

The spread of the monasteries, and hence of monastic libraries, was greatly encouraged by establishment of the various orders of monks. The Benedictine
order, one of the earliest, was particularly interested
in books and learning, and each of their branch monasteries was required to have a library. The Augustin-
ians and the Dominicans were also great lovers of
books, and their libraries ranked second only to those
of the Benedictines. The libraries of the Cistercians
were designed wholly to assist in their religious
studies, and hence contained almost no secular literature, but those of the Carthusians were more wordly
and as much as a third of their works might treat non-
religious subjects.

Whatever its order, the monastery usually included
special quarters for its library and scriptorium. The
latter was the work-room, where books were copied,
illuminated and bound. The "scriptores" or writers
sat or stood at sloping desks, and copied, hour after
hour, as another monk read to them. Or, if only one
copy was desired, the copyist would be his own reader.
After the text was copied, the pages went on to artist-
monks who illuminated or illustrated the books with
ornamental drawings for initial capital letters, and a-
long the borders of the pages. If these illuminations
were in red, as they often were, they were termed
"rubrications," and the artist was a "rubricator."
Other colors were used, however, including gold and
silver. In some of the more elaborate manuscripts,
the parchment itself was tinted. The art of book illumination reached a high level during the later middle
ages, but many of the earlier works were also noted
for their beauty. The Book of Kells, a copy of the
four Gospels produced at an Irish monastery in the
seventh century, has been called one of the most
beautiful books ever made. The bindings of the
books produced in the monasteries also reached near
perfection, being made of fine leathers and textiles,
sometimes even of velvet. For very large books, the
backs were made of wood covered with leather, and
fastened with metal clasps. The leather bindings were
ornamented with fancy toolings, either blind or with
colors or gold foil pressed into the embossings. The
more valuable books were chained to the tables or

lecterns upon which they lay, and all reading had to be done standing up.

In the monastery libraries the books continued, throughout much of the Middle Ages, to be kept in chests rather than on shelves. This was a carry-over from the days of the vellum rolls, which had usually been kept in chests. Monks were assigned to care for the books, including repairs to the volumes, and records of the numbers and titles. A number of medieval monastery catalogs, or lists of books, have been preserved. The books of the Bible, usually divided into several separate volumes, were always present, often in many copies. Next in importance came the commentaries on the Bible, and the lives of the saints. The early Christian writings were usually present, with St. Augustine being a favorite, and his City of God being probably the most popular single work other than the Bible. Only a minor part of the monastery library was given over to secular works. Among these were books of law, philosophy, science, medicine, and occasionally a few books on magic. Only a few of the classic authors were present, but Seneca, Cicero and Aristotle were known, at least for a part of their works. Each monastery may have contained some works on local history and writings of local authors but for the most part the monastery library of England was apt to be very similar to that of France, Germany or Italy. Sometimes secular works were preserved unintentionally when the parchment on which they were written was washed or erased and a religious work written over it. The original writing would not be completely obliterated, and could later be read after special treatment. Such accidentally preserved manuscripts are called palimpsests.

The usual method of acquisition for monastery libraries was by copying. A manuscript could sometimes be borrowed for copying, but usually a monk would be sent from one monastery to another to copy literary treasures. Sometimes such trips would take a monk from Ireland to Spain or from Poland to Italy, just to obtain a copy of a needed work. Copies of the more popular works could be bought but the monks seldom had the funds. Many monastery libraries were increased substantially through gifts and through bequests, either from wealthy merchants and nobles, or from religious leaders who had collected private libraries. As collections of books grew larger, methods of separating and arranging the books had to be devised. Usually this arrangement began by dividing the religious from the secular works, and then the works in Greek from those in Latin. When further division was made, it was roughly by subject, with all the books in a particular field being kept in the same chest. Sometimes the division was by size, or even by source, when a special gift collection was kept together. Ordinarily the books in the monastery library were available only to the monks or their students, and except for texts, they had to be used in the reading room, but occasionally an important religious or political official could borrow volumes for his own use.

In the midst of the Dark Ages, the reign of the Frankish emperor, Charlemagne, (742-814) stands out as far as books and learning is concerned. Charlemagne himself was something of a scholar and he felt a need to improve and spread learning in order to hold his large and sprawling empire together. He gathered a personal library of note, but he is mainly remembered for the palace library which he directed to be collected, not only from his realm, but from other lands. Important works in Italy and Spain were copied for Charlemagne's library, and works already there were edited and compared with others to test their authenticity and to remove interpolations of over-enthusiastic copyists. The style of writing was improved during this period, and a new script, usually called the Carolingian minuscule, was developed, and remained a standard for several hundred years. The term Carolingian came from the Latin form of Charlemagne's name, while minuscule identified the script as being composed of small letters rather than the majuscule or capital letters in general use since the days of the Romans. The influence of this premature renaissance spread, and scholars from Greece to Britain came to Tours to consult the palace library.

Among the scholars attracted to Charlemagne's court was the distinguished English monk, Alcuin (735-804).

Alcuin had founded and developed the monastery library
at York, England, and had become renowned as a religious leader and teacher. Charlemagne first called on
Alcuin to direct a school which had grown up around
his library at Tours. This school, which seems to
have been something of a public college, was a fore-
runner of later medieval universities. Upon the success
of this educational venture, Charlemagne encouraged the
establishment of similar schools throughout his realm,
which then included most of western Europe. Alcuin
advised that if a library and scriptorium were established at any given place, a school would naturally
grow up around it. Later Alcuin became the abbot at
St. Martin of Tours, and there he established a model
library for a religious institution. He made his church
library something of a source library, where standard
texts were kept for copying by anyone who could visit
or who could pay a copyist. Charlemagne and Alcuin
stand out in the field of library history, but like others
before them, their efforts did not long survive them.
With the feudal wars and Viking invasions that swept
much of western Europe in the ninth and tenth centuries, many of these libraries were destroyed, and the
spirit that built them was quiescent for several hundred
years.

In the eleventh and twelfth centuries the monasteries
of Germany and central Europe were active in building
and preserving libraries, especially those at Fulda,
Corvey, St. Gall and Regensburg. In these institutions,
which were for the most part schools as well as monasteries, the position of librarius became established as
the custodian of the books. It was the duty of this official to arrange the books, to see that sufficient
copies of the more important texts were available, to
keep records of use, and, in general, to carry out the
usual functions of a librarian. The library cooperated
closely with the scriptorium, and books borrowed from
other monasteries could be copied for the collection.
Illumination and book-bindings reached their height during these centuries, and many of the manuscript volumes
that have survived from these collections are truly
works of art. Closely akin to the monastery library
was the cathedral library which flourished after about
the tenth century. The cathedral library at Canterbury

in England is said to have had more than 3000 volumes
in the twelfth century, and if this is true it must have
been extraordinarily large for its time. Most of the
medieval monastery and cathedral libraries, of which
records have survived, numbered their literary
treasures in the hundreds, rather than thousands. Of
course, it must be remembered that these bound
volumes contained ten or twenty times as much written
matter as the classic papyrus roll, and this must be
considered in comparing the size of the medieval libraries with those of the ancients.

In considering the intellectual history of medieval
Europe, the Moslem civilization in Spain and Portugal
should not be ignored. Following the conquest of that
area by the Moors in the eighth century, a highly developed, civilization emerged, and cities such as Toledo,
Seville and Cordova became centers of learning. The
University of Cordova in the tenth century was one of
the three great Moslem universities, and there were
lesser colleges at several other Spanish cities. No less
than seventy important libraries were recorded in Spain
during the tenth to twelfth centuries, many of them
filled with rare and beautiful books. The technique of
paper-making entered western Europe through Spain, as
did also the ornate Morocco leather book bindings. The
Spanish Moslems were not only collectors of books, but
they were writers as well, and produced many of the
important medieval works in science and philosophy.
By the late twelfth century, however, Moslem civilization in Spain was on the decline, and there were political and religious leaders who ordered that books be destroyed, and that all writing contrary to the prevailing
religious beliefs should be banned. In the remainder of
western Europe, at about the same time, the monastery
libraries were also entering into a period of decline,
but their place was being taken on the cultural stage by
the development of the medieval university and its
libraries.

From the fall of Rome to the twelfth century, for the
most part, education in western Europe was in the hands
of the monasteries. Most of the instruction in these religious schools was theological, but it was usual for the
monks to give the rudiments of schooling to the sons of

neighboring noblemen, and sometimes to promising children of poorer folk. Some of the monastic orders encouraged education for all, and during the reigns of monarchs like Charlemagne, the wide development of schools was encouraged. Then, too, in some of the trading centers, schools grew up to train clerks for the growing business firms. Reading, writing and a-rithmetic were about the fullest extent of their studies. Whether in monastery or trade school, lessons were memorized and recited by rote; independent thought or reading was not encouraged. By the late eleventh centu-ry, however, some of these secular schools were reach-ing higher levels of instruction, and in some cases, as in Paris, degrees of bachelor of arts were granted for the completion of a given series of studies. The ca-thedral school, which to some extent replaced the monastery as a teaching center in the eleventh century, followed in the steps of its predecessor, teaching the fundamentals of a liberal education centered around the Latin Bible. A few great scholars emerged from these schools (including John of Salisbury (d.1180), at Canter-bury, and Peter Abelard (1079-1142) in Paris) but for the most part the educational level of both teachers and pupils was mediocre.

The development of the medieval universities, how-ever, changed this pattern and raised the level of learn-ing in western Europe to a point where the Renaissance could begin. The earliest universities of renown were those in northern Italy, and these grew largely out of law schools, established for the study of both civil and religious law. Later, universities in northern Europe grew in much the same way from cathedral schools. In either case, the university of the later middle ages was in reality a group of teachers, formed into something of a guild, each teaching a different subject, and empower-ed, by political or religious powers or both, to grant degrees. A student usually studied under one teacher alone until he felt that he had learned all he could from that source, and then went on to another. Before a de-gree could be received, however, an examination before a group of the masters or teachers had to be passed. Early universities of renown were at Bologna, Padua and Paris.

In these early universities there were no libraries
as such at first. Each master had a collection of
books which he might lend or rent to his students.
Each student in turn had to provide not only his own
text-books, but anything else that he might wish to read,
unless he could borrow or rent it from a master or
book-seller. Only the most wealthy of students could
afford to own all the texts he might wish to study, so
the book rental trade was brisk. Usually the university
authorities controlled the book trade in order to guaran-
tee the authenticity of the texts and the book-sellers or
"stationarii" were licensed by them, as were also the
dealers in parchment and other writing materials.

As the universities grew in numbers of students, and
as they came to include several colleges, the demand
for books made it necessary to establish libraries.
Usually each college had its own library, and at the
University of Paris the outstanding college library was
that of the Sorbonne, which by 1322 contained over a
thousand volumes. By 1400, the Sorbonne library had
established a circulating library, consisting of duplicates and books of lesser value, which could be taken
from the library by the students after the payment of a
deposit. By 1480, this library was housed in a separate building, with a main reading room twelve by forty
feet. While the more important books were still chained to the shelves, the chains had been lengthened so that
the weary student could take his book to a nearby table.
A set of rules for the use of the Sorbonne library has
been preserved. Some of them may sound odd, but
most of them are still familiar. A few of these rules
(adapted from Nathan Schachner, The Medieval Universities, p. 329) were :

No student could enter the library unless wearing
cap and gown.

Each member (student) of the college had a key to
the library, and no one else could enter the library
except with a member.

It was forbidden to write on the volumes, or tear
out leaves.

As far as possible, silence was to reign in the library.

Books containing condemned doctrines could be read only by professors of theology, and then only when necessary.

In organization, the university library was similar to the larger monastery libraries, except that instead of being divided into secular and religious works, the books were divided into groups according to the subjects or faculties taught in the colleges. Within these groups there were apparently no sub-classes, and books were arranged according to size and accession. In handling the books, the transition from chests to lecterns and bookshelves was a gradual one, but by the end of the middle ages, the shelves were in common use. Lists of books in the college libraries were usually kept by subject groups, and within those groups by titles. Also, there was sometimes a finding list of books arranged as they were on the shelves. In the Sorbonne Library, the different faculties were distinguished by colors, with each book marked with its color, and sometimes with additional letters or numbers to indicate the shelf or section where it was kept.

In addition to the early universities at Paris and in Italy, other notable ones with important libraries were those at Prague (1366); Heidelberg (1386); Oxford (1412); and Cambridge (1425). The dates given are those in which libraries are known to have been functioning and not necessarily those of the founding of the university. At Oxford, Richard de Bury had planned a college library as early as 1345, and with his own collection of books as a nucleus a library was founded at Durham College, Oxford, shortly afterward. Unfortunately, Durham College was later dissolved and its books scattered. De Bury himself, a leading religious figure and Bishop of Durham, was an ardent book collector. At several times in his life he made long trips through Europe to collect manuscripts for his library. His account of why and how he collected books is told in his Philobiblon, or, The Love of Books. Closely related to the early English university libraries was the Guildhall Library, formed in London by Lord Mayor Richard Whittington early in the fifteenth century. This library was open to all scholars and students.

As the Middle Ages progressed and declined, a few important private libraries were founded in larger cities of Europe. Among them were those of the Italian writers Petrarch and Boccaccio, and of the Medici family. About 1440, the Medicis gave from their own private library enough books to start a library in San Marco that has been called the first public library in Italy. Federigo, Duke of Urbino, founded the famous Urbino Library of Greek and Roman classics in the fifteenth century, largely by gifts from his own private library. For both Federigo and the Medicis, Vespasiano de Bisticci (1421-1498) served as book agent and collector. Vespasiano was something of a scholar and editor, and kept a staff of copyists busy making copies of important works which he found in his travels through Europe. In Hungary, King Matthias Corvinus was reported to have a library of more than 50,000 manuscripts which was destroyed by the Turks in their invasion of Europe. Charles V of France, in the 14th century, amassed a very large collection of books which were arranged and cataloged by a full-time librarian. Another French ruler, Philip the Good, Duke of Burgundy, set out to acquire the largest and finest library in the world, and maintained a regular staff of scholars, translators, calligraphers and illuminators to build up his collection. Many private collectors donated their libraries to universities. Robert de Sorbonne, in 1250, gave his collection to the college that took his name in Paris; and Duke Humphrey of Gloucester, gave his library to Oxford in the early fifteenth century. Many of the medieval libraries, whether private, religious or university, were later destroyed or scattered in political and religious wars, but many more have survived as treasured collections in modern libraries.

One library of the Middle Ages that deserves special notice was the Library of the Popes in the Vatican at Rome. Tradition has it that the early popes had begun a Vatican library even before the end of the Roman empire, but the history of these early papal libraries is obscure. We know that there was a papal library at least from the sixth century on, and that particularly under Pope Zacharias (741-752) it received important accessions from the earlier monastery libraries. Because of the struggles within the Church in the 13th and 14th centuries few if any of its original treasures were preserved. A new Vatican library was begun in the early 15th century, and this library grew into importance under the direction of Pope Nicholas V (1447-1455), who himself had been a librarian and had cataloged the Medici library at San Marco. By 1500, the Vatican library contained more than a thousand volumes, not counting duplicates, and was divided into a private library for the Pope and the main library for the use of the monks and scholars. The papal library served as the central library of the Roman Catholic Church, and as such it preserved the most authoritative texts of all the major Christian writings. Copies of religious works were made continuously for distribution to churches and monasteries throughout the Catholic world, and duplicates were kept for loan or deposit in other church libraries. Though the Vatican library never reached great size before the modern era, the quality and value of its holdings were particularly high and made it one of the most important libraries in the world.

An important adjunct of the medieval library was the commercial book maker and bookseller. Although the majority of books were in the hands of religious or official libraries, there were private book collectors, and there was business to be carried on in providing books for libraries, schools and scholars, particularly after the tenth century. The professional copyists, the book publishers of their day, could not rival the monks in the accuracy or artistic perfection of their works, but they could compete in school texts. Also, the private book makers did produce and sell much of the secular literature of the day--although there was comparatively little of it. The copyist usually flourished in the towns, and by the later middle ages he could be found, usually along with book-binders and illuminators, in an organized company or guild. The medieval book-seller, on the other hand, was often a lone hand, although he might have agents in distant cities. Usually he could be found in the larger towns, or around universities and monasteries, often adding to his income by renting books to students who could not afford to buy their own texts. In 1323, there were no less than 28 book-sellers in the vicinity of the University of Paris, some of them offering as many as 125 texts for rent. On a higher level, commercially speaking, were the international book-dealers, sometimes really smugglers, who could obtain for a Paris customer a rare text from Constantinople or Cordova, and who handled books and manuscripts in the same manner that they would costly fabrics or works of art. Some of these book men, as for example, Vespasiano, were scholars themselves, and by securing the texts of the classics from the East and making them available in Western Europe they contributed substantially to the beginning of the Renaissance.

Even ordinary books in the Middle Ages were luxuries. It has been estimated that in current values, an average volume in the 12th century would have sold for about two hundred dollars. Many relatively wealthy and scholarly people acquired only a few books in a lifetime, and wills have been preserved that mention twenty or thirty books as a valuable bequest. There are records of a Bible being traded for a house and lot that would today sell for ten thousand dollars or more, and a Missal being traded for an extensive vineyard. Markets for such items were limited, of course, and there were few who had both the wealth and the interest to acquire many books. However, despite the scarcity of books and the smallness of medieval libraries, the fact remains that the cultural centers of the Middle Ages did bridge the gap between the ancient and the modern worlds. Despite the ravages of wars and time, copies of the classics and of contemporary writing were preserved, and today we consider them a most important part of the heritage of the western world.

Bibliography

Addison, Julia D.: Arts and crafts in the Middle Ages. Philadelphia, 1908. 398 p. (See especially pp.326-364.)

Beddie, J.S.: Libraries in the twelfth century; their catalogs and contents. Boston, 1929. 23 p.

Bradley, John W.: Illustrated manuscripts. London, 1905. 290 p.

Brassington, William S.: A history of the art of bookbinding with some account of the books of the ancients London, 1894. 270 p.

Clark, J.W.: The care of books. Cambridge, England, 1902. 352 p.

------ Libraries in the medieval and renaissance periods. Cambridge, England, 1894. 61 p.

Davenport, Cyril: The book, its history and development. New York, 1930. 258 p. (See p. 26-61.)

De Bury, Richard: Philiobiblon, or, The Love of books. London, 1925. 148 p.

Durant, Will: The age of faith. New York, 1950. 1196 p.

Graham, Hugh: Early Irish monastic schools. Dublin, 1923. 206 p.

Guppy, Henry: Stepping stones to the art of typography. London, 1928. 45 p.

Hamilton, Frederick W.: Books before typography. Chicago, 1918. 47 p.

Herbert, John A.: Illuminated manuscripts. London, 1912. 135 p.

Hessel, Alfred: A history of libraries. New Brunswick, 1955. 198 p. (See pp. 9-37.)

Hind, A.M.: An introduction to the history of woodcut. New York, 1935. 2 vols.

Johnston, Edward: Writing and illuminating and lettering. New York, 1939. 500 p.

Holzknecht, Karl J.: Literary patronage in the Middle Ages. Philadelphia, 1923. 258 p.

Laurie, S.S.: The rise and early constitution of the universities. New York, 1891. 293 p.

Lipsius, Justus: A brief outline of the history of libraries. Chicago, 1907. 121 p.

Madan, Falconer: Books in manuscript. London, 1920. 208 p.

Mason, William A.: A history of the art of writing. New York, 1928. 502 p. (See especially pp. 392-441.)

Merryweather, Frederick: Bibliomania in the Middle Ages. New York, 1900. 322 p.

Meyer, Kuno: Learning in Ireland in the fifth century. Dublin, 1913. 29 p.

Middleton, J.H.: Illuminated manuscripts in classical and medieval times. Cambridge, England. 1892. 270 p

Muir, P.H.: Talks on book collecting. London, 1952. 105 p. (See especially pp. 25-39 on "The period before printing.")

Orcutt, W.D.: In quest of the perfect book. Boston, 1926. (See especially pp. 109-150.)

Putnam, G.H.: Authors and their public in ancient times. New York, 1896. 326 p.

------ Books and their makers during the Middle Ages. New York, 1896. 2 vols.

Savage, Ernest A.: Old English libraries; the making, collecting and use of books during the Middle Ages. London, 1911. 298 p.

Schachner, Nathan: The medieval university. New York 1938. 388 p.

Simon, Howard: 500 years of art in illustration. New York, 1942. 476 p.

Taylor, Archer: Renaissance guides to books. Berkeley, Calif. 1925. 130 p.

Ullman, B.L.: Ancient writing and its influence. New York, 1932. 234 p.

Weitenkampf, Frank : The illustrated book. Cambridge, England, 1938. 264 p.

West, Andrew: Alcuin and the rise of the Christian schools. New York, 1892. 205 p.

- - - - - -

Beddie, J.S.: Ancient classics in the medieval libraries. Speculum, V, (1930), 3-20.

Mackensen, Ruth S.: "Four great libraries of medieval Baghdad." Library Quarterly, II, (1932), 279-299.

Root, Robert K.: "Publication before printing." Modern Language Association, Publications, XXVIII, (1913), 417-431.

Schutz, Geza, "Bibliotheca Corvina," Library Quarterly, IV, (1934), 552-563.

IV Early Printing

The fifteenth century saw the coming of the second most important event in the history of books and libraries. The first, of course, was the development of writing; the second, the development of printing. Ordinarily we say that Johann Gutenberg invented printing about 1450. However, there is much more to the story than that; there were others involved besides Gutenberg, and we should say "printing from movable type" in order to be reasonably correct about the date. Actually, if we define printing in its simplest form as making an impression of intelligible characters by one object upon another, then printing began long before the Christian era. The Babylonians and Egyptians used metal or wooden seals for impressing pictures and pictographs upon clay or wax. The Babylonians even used a seal-cylinder, by means of which an entire paragraph could be rolled out on a clay tablet with one turn of the embossed cylinder. The Chinese in the fifth and sixth centuries A.D. used similar seals, inked, for the printing of short mottoes and charms. In 770 A.D., a small book of Buddhist charms was produced in this manner in Japan and hundreds of copies were placed in shrines throughout the country. This is sometimes called the first printed book.

A somewhat better claim to the first printing comes from China, where the carved seal developed into the full-page woodcut. This carefully carved wooden block could contain an illustration and a half page or more of Chinese characters, thus presenting the appearance of a modern book page. By the ninth century, A.D., the Chinese were producing books in this manner, and a copy of one of them, the "Diamond Sutra" printed in 868, has survived. A "sutra" was a Buddhist holy book, and this particular one was printed on a roll sixteen feet long and one foot wide. By the tenth century, printing in this manner was fairly common in China.

The Chinese not only originated block printing, but also an elementary form of printing from movable type. Since the Chinese written language was based on a phonetic syllabary rather than an alphabet, one piece of type could be used to print a whole word. Experiments with individual pieces of type for each character, with the type made of baked clay, were made as early as the eleventh century. These types were locked together in a wooden form, inked and pressed upon the paper much in the manner of later printing. Two centuries later the Chinese printers were trying movable types made of tin and wood, but printing from wood blocks remained the usual form of duplicating written materials in China, and the movable type did not gain acceptance. Korea borrowed printing from movable metal type from the Chinese, and by the early fifteenth century, still long before Gutenberg, the Koreans were printing hundreds of copies of books from movable type. But the Koreans, like the Chinese, used type slugs containing a whole word rather than a single letter, so they fell short of the workable system later developed in Europe, and printing in Korea fell into disuse in the same century that saw it rise. There are examples of printing from movable types in China and Japan in the sixteenth and seventeenth centuries, but most printing in those countries continued to be done from woodblocks.

The knowledge of wood-block printing spread gradually westward from China, possibly as far as Egypt, but not, as far as we know, to western Europe. One interesting form in which the block printing spread was that of playing cards. The origin of card games is undoubtedly Chinese, where they were first called "sheet dice." They were used there in the tenth century, and probably even earlier. Block printed playing cards were in use in Europe by the fourteenth century, although any direct connection between the European cards and their Chinese ancestors is difficult to trace. It is generally felt, however, that the idea of block printing probably spread westward with the game of cards. Block printing was also used in the Asiatic countries between China and Europe for printing money, charms and brief sacred writings from the twelfth to the fifteen century.

Whether or not there is a definite connection between early printing in Europe and that developed in China, there is no doubt about the spread of another phase of book-making from East to West. This was the manufacture of paper. Papyrus, parchment and vellum were all comparatively expensive, and for a process that made hundreds of copies of a work in a short time, a cheaper material was necessary. Many materials had been tried in various countries for use in writing-- wood, clay, stone, metal, hides, cloth, papyrus-- but all were either too scarce or too bulky for use in mechanical printing. Several primitive peoples, including natives of the Southwest Pacific and of Mexico, developed sheets of matted vegetable fibers that were primitive forms of paper, but the Chinese first made useable paper. As early as the second century, A.D., the Chinese experimented with paper made from silk, tree bark and hemp. Later cotton and linen rags were used for paper making, and by the fifth century, paper was common in China. This paper was made by soaking and pounding the raw materials until the individual fibres were separated. A thick solution was made of water and fibres, and then a fine meshed screen was dipped into the mixture. As the screen was lifted a thin layer of the fibres adhered to the screen, and when this was dried and peeled off, it made a single sheet of paper. Later the paper was pressed and sometimes rubbed with stone to give it a smooth hard finish.

Traveling westward along the trade routes, the use of paper had reached Persia by the eighth century, and Baghdad by the ninth. Egypt used paper by the tenth century, the Moslems in Spain in the eleventh or twelfth, and the south Italians by the thirteenth. Paper was not actually made in north Europe until the fifteenth century, and not in England until nearly 1500. The oldest extant European paper document came from Sicily and was dated 1209. Fabriano in Italy had the earliest known paper mill in Europe in 1270, but in the fourteenth and fifteenth centuries the French became the most important paper makers in Europe. Rag, whether of cotton, linen, hemp or silk, continued to be the main raw materials for paper, and wood pulp did not come into use until the nineteenth century. Oddly enough, paper did not receive a warm welcome in Europe, despite its comparative cheapness as a writing material. Religious and governmental leaders opposed its use, particularly on important documents, and for many years it was illegal to use paper for official manuscripts.

Just as printing began in the Far East with impressions made from block, so it was the wood-block print that first was used in Europe. By around 1400 playing cards were being made by this method, and also small cards with religious figures on them. From these it was only a short step to the block book, with small pages each printed from a single block. As in the Far East, these pages usually consisted of a large picture and a small number of words. The earliest known European block books dated from around 1428, although separate prints have been found that were probably produced earlier. The block book was usually on a religious theme, such as the Pauper's Bible, a series of short illustrated sermons, or it was a school book, generally a Latin grammar. Several hundred different works were produced in this form during the fifteenth century, many of them after the introduction of regular printing. The block books were primarily intended for the poorer reading public, and as such they were apparently well-used, for only a few examples of them survive as compared to the thousands of early printed books still preserved.

In order to discuss the role of Johann Gutenberg in the invention of printing, it is necessary to know a little about the man himself. He was born about 1400 in Mainz, Germany, and seems to have come from a fairly wealthy family. About 1430 he left Mainz and took up his home in Strasbourg, where he entered into a partnership with several craftsmen, workers in gold and other metals. During his years in Strasbourg, Gutenberg became involved in several lawsuits, both in business and domestic matters (he was sued for breach of promise by one Strasbourg lady), and thus his presence there is a matter of record. However, just when he began work on a printing press is uncertain. About 1440, he was sued by two of his ex-partners for failing to teach them a secret process, un-named but usually thought to have been printing. There are a few fragments of printing which some authorities believe were printed by Gutenberg in Strasbourg, but there is no general agreement on these. In 1448, however, Gutenberg was back in Mainz, and by 1450 he was definitely in the printing business as several of his contemporaries later recorded. In 1452, already indebted to one Johann Fust, Gutenberg took that gentleman into partnership with him. By this time, the press was in operation, but apparently it brought little remuneration to Gutenberg, for by 1455 he was so indebted to Fust that he made over his share of the printing equipment to Fust and another partner, Peter Schoeffer. From this press, the work of Gutenberg but the property of Fust and Schoeffer, there came in 1456 the famous Gutenberg Bible, sometimes called the 42-line Bible from the number of lines of type per page. This edition of the Bible was no experimental affair; it is undoubtedly one of the finest pieces of printing ever done. It does not seem logical that a first printed book could be such an example of perfection, so it must be assumed that many years of experimentation and trial and error were necessary before a printing press could be developed to do such fine work. Apparently those years of experiment without income impoverished Gutenberg, and his creditors and business successors reaped the benefits of his work.

No single piece of printing actually bears the imprint of Gutenberg, but from careful study of the available records most authorities agree in crediting him with several items, and of course it is quite possible that dozens of minor books, pamphlets and broadsides may have been printed by Gutenberg, but lost in the years after his death. The first dated piece of printing was an indulgence, a broadside church form, printed in 1454, apparently by a Gutenberg press in the hands of Peter Schoeffer. The 42-line Bible was probably printed in 1454 or 1455, because, although it bears no date itself, a copy was illuminated and bound by Heinrich Cremer in the summer of 1456, according to a note in a copy surviving in the Bibliothéque Nationale in Paris. This so-called Gutenberg Bible was most probably completed by Fust and Schoeffer, but the press, the type and possibly even the composition of the Bible were Gutenberg's handiwork.

Did Gutenberg really invent the printing press? The best evidence indicates that he did. At least he put together the first workable press using movable metal type, and developed it mechanically to the point where excellent printing could be achieved. A skilled metalworker, he was perfectly capable of designing and casting the type; the ink was available from that used with wood-cuts, although some adaptation was probably necessary; and the press itself was the screw-press, long used in wine-making and leather-curing. The combination of these necessary elements, however, did constitute an invention, and its perfection was a notable achievement. When Gutenberg died and where he is buried is still a mystery, but despite questions surrounding his life and work, he is given credit for developing the first practical printing press, in the German city of Mainz, around 1450.

Other European cities also claim the invention of printing. The Netherlands in particular have a case for Laurence Koster, who is alleged to have used a printing press with movable type as early as 1430. There is little proof to support this claim, although there is evidence that someone was experimenting with printing from movable type in the Netherlands about the same time that Gutenberg was developing his press. One other interesting claimant to Gutenberg's fame has come from France, where in 1444-1446 at Avignon, one Procopius Waldfoghel, a silver smith, was experimenting with "alphabets of steel," with which he claimed to be able to "write artificially." There is no evidence to show that Waldfoghel ever did any actual printing. Other, even more vague and unsubstantiated claims to the invention of printing come from other cities in France, and from Germany, Italy and Czechoslovakia. Until and unless some more substantial discovery is made in the field of early printing, Gutenberg's position seems secure.

Though some may question the inventor of printing, there seems to be little doubt that the first successful printing did begin in the city of Mainz in the mid-fifteenth century, and that it did spread from that city to the rest of Europe. In 1462 a feudal war between two competing claimants for the archbishopric of Mainz resulted in the capture of that city by one force and the complete disruption of the printing industry there. Some printers, out of work at least temporarily, had to look elsewhere for employment. Some were probably forced to leave because they had opposed the victorious bishop. At any rate, printers who had been trained in the shops of Gutenberg, Fust and Schoeffer, spread out after 1462 and carried their knowledge of printing to other parts of Europe. A French writer described this exodus in 1470:

There has been discovered in Germany a wonderful new method for the production of books, and those who have mastered this method are taking their invention from Mainz out into the world somewhat as the old Grecian warriors took their weapons from the belly of the Trojan horse. The light of this wonderful discovery will spread to all parts of the earth. (Putnam, G.H.: Books and their makers during the middle ages, I, 359.)

It was natural that the nearby German towns should receive printing shortly after it had been perfected in Mainz, and this seems to have been the case. There were printers in Strasbourg by 1460, in Bamberg by 1461, and in Cologne by 1465 or earlier. Some of the German printers crossed the Alps and began the first presses in Italy. Conrad Sweynheym and Arnold Pannartz left Mainz and began a printing establishment at Subiaco, near Rome, either late in 1464 or early in 1465. Later they moved on to Rome and became the first printers in that city. Other Italian cities had printing presses in the 1470's, including Venice, where the industry flourished, Naples, Florence and Genoa. Basel in Switzerland had printing by 1468, Paris in 1470, the Netherlands shortly afterward, and even Cracow, Poland, by 1475. The art was slower in reaching the Baltic countries and the Balkans, and it was not until the 1480's that there were presses in Denmark, Norway and Sweden, and not until 1494 that printing reached Constantinople. The first printing in England was done in 1476 or early in 1477, and in Spain in 1474. There were reports of three printers going to Moscow in 1490, but there is no record of any actual printing by them, and there are no known Russian incunabula. The first known printing in Moscow was not done until 1553.

In the last quarter of the fifteenth century, the art of printing spread to all the major cities of Europe, and many printers became outstanding in their profession. Italy early assumed the lead, and among the early Italian printers Nicholas Jenson and Aldus Manutius stand out. Jenson is particularly known for his fine printing done in Venice in a clear, very legible type called "Roman," with which he produced more than 150 different books. Just as Gutenberg's type had been based on the gothic handwriting then prevalent in Germany, so Jenson based his roman type on the script used by the humanist scholars of northern Italy. Aldus Manutius, also of Venice, was known for his development of italic type, and for the printing, in small, well-made but relatively cheap editions, of the Greek and Latin classics. Most early printers preferred the folio format for their books, but Aldus turned to the octavo, a small, hand-sized volume that was easy to hold and read. Most modern books are in the octavo size. More than any other of the early printers, Jenson and Aldus were responsible for popularizing the printed book, and thus helping to spread learning. Both men were scholars as well as printers and edited the books they published. One of the greatest achievements of Aldus Manutius was the collection of the many fragments of Aristotle's works into as nearly complete an edition of his writings as was then possible. He is also remembered for the founding of the Aldine Academy for the study of the Greek and Latin classics, but this did not survive long after his death in 1515.

Among the early German printers, the Koberger family of Nuremberg stands out for the quantity if not the quality of their work. They printed on a large scale, running several presses, with a number of workmen, each trained in a special task. They tended to specialize in religious works and in text-books, and by 1500 had twenty-four presses in operation in Nuremberg and nearby towns. Many of their books were profusely illustrated with wood-cuts. One of the Kobergers' most

48

famous works is the Nuremberg Chronicle, which was
an illustrated history of the world. It was very elaborate, with almost two thousand illustrations, but it was
so carelessly done that the same wood-cut was often
used several times to depict different people or different scenes. The Kobergers promoted their business
effectively with published catalogs and salesmen who
peddled their books throughout Europe. Johann Snell,
of Lubeck, Germany, had a similar establishment with
branches in Denmark and Sweden.

Among other fifteenth and sixteenth century European
printers of importance were several generations of the
Estienne family of France. Beginning with Henri
Estienne in 1490, and for more than 150 years, this
family produced, in Paris and Geneva, some of the
finest books ever published. Another famous printing
family was the House of Plantin, in Antwerp, which
lasted for some 300 years, and was noted for excellent
printing from the sixteenth to the nineteenth century.
The Elzevir press, in Leiden, produced over 1600 books
in five different languages in a little over a century of
operation. Switzerland considers Johann Froben, who
printed in Basel from 1491 to 1527, one of its greatest
printers. Froben surrounded himself with scholars, including Erasmus, and undertook to produce only the
best of printing and the most authentic of texts. Among
his most notable publications was a Greek New Testament, edited by Erasmus, and the works of St. Jerome
in nine huge folio volumes. Froben also published
some of the earliest works on medicine and science,
part of which were illustrated with wood-cuts by Hans
Holbein.

Closely associated with printing throughout its history
has been the art of type-founding. Early printers like
Gutenberg and Jenson were also type-founders, and they
took their type designs from the most prevalent and
most scholarly hand writing in their respective areas.
By the sixteenth century, however, type designing and
founding was becoming a separate trade, and types were
being created specifically for printing. Two Frenchmen
stand out for their contribution to type designs in the
sixteenth century. One of these was Robert Granjon,
who specialized in italic typefaces, and the other was

Claude Garamond, who developed a clear, open roman character, based somewhat on the Jenson type. Both styles of type were widely used by contemporary printers, and after a revival of interest in them in the nineteenth century are still popular.

Printing was relatively late in reaching England, with the first printing there coming late in 1476, or early 1477. The first English printer was William Caxton, a wealthy merchant who had been living in Bruges, Belgium. He apparently learned the art during a visit to Cologne, Germany, and took it up at first as a hobby. At the request of Margaret, Duchess of Burgundy, who was English born, Caxton had translated from the French a popular book on the Trojan wars, entitled Recuyell of the Hystoryes of Troye, and he printed some copies of this in Bruges about 1475. Thus the first book printed in English was not printed in England. Caxton decided that printing could be a profitable trade, and so in 1476, he returned to England and set up his printing business at Westminster Abbey. There his first dated printing was another translation, The Dictes or Sayengis of the Philosophers, 1477. There were probably earlier publications in pamphlet or broadside form from the Caxton press, but none of them has survived. Before his death in 1491, Caxton printed more than a hundred different works, including the poems of Geoffrey Chaucer, who was virtually a contemporary. As a printer, Caxton was not an artist, and his works fall short of perfection, but as an editor and publisher he did help to standardize the English language and preserve its literature. Caxton used several type-faces at different times, but the one for which he is best remembered is the Old English black-letter, a heavy, almost Gothic type that is still sometimes used.

Table I The Spread of Printing in Europe

Date	Country	City	Printer
1445-1453 (?)	Germany	Mainz	Johann Gutenberg
1454	Germany	Mainz	Fust and Schoeffer
1458-1460 (?)	Germany	Strasbourg	Johann Mentelin
1461	Germany	Bamberg	Albrecht Pfister
1464-1465 (?)	Italy	Subiaco	Sweynheym and Pannartz
1465	Germany	Cologne	Ulrich Zell
1467	Italy	Rome	Sweynheym and Pannartz
1468	Germany	Augsburg	Gunther Zainer
1468 (?)	Switzerland	Basel	Berthold Ruppel
1468	Czechoslovakia	Pilsen	(Unknown)
1469	Italy	Venice	John of Spires
1470	Germany	Nuremberg	Johann Sensenschmid.
1470 (?)	Italy	Venice	Nicolas Jenson
1470	France	Paris	Martin Crantz, Ulrich Gering, Michael Friburger.
1470	Netherlands	Utrecht	Gerardus Leempt and Nicholaus Ketalaer
1471	Italy	Milan	Antonio Zarotti
1471	Italy	Naples	Sixtus Riessinger
1471	Italy	Florence	Bernardo di Cennini
1473	France	Lyons	Wilhelm Konig
1473-1474 (?)	Hungary	Budapest	Andreas Hesse
1473-1474	Belgium	Louvain	John of Westphalia
1474	Poland	Cracow	Caspar Hochfelder
1474	Spain	Valencia	Lambert Palmart
1476-1477	England	Westminster	William Caxton

Date	Country	City	Printer
1478	England	Oxford	Theodoric Rood
1480	England	London	John Lettou
1482	Austria	Vienna	Stephan Koblinger
1482	Denmark	Odensee	Johann Snell
1489	Portugal	Lisbon	Rabbi Elieser
1490	England	London	Richard Pynson
1491	England	Westminster	Wynkyn de Worde
1491	Switzerland	Basel	Johann Froben
1494	Turkey	Constantinople	David ibn Nachmias
1494	Italy	Venice	Aldus Manutius
1502	France	Paris	Henri Estienne
1515	France	Paris	Geoffrey Tory
1549	Belgium	Antwerp	Christopher Plantin

Caxton's successor was Wynken de Worde, who had
been his assistant almost from the first. Wynken de
Worde was in many ways a better printer than Caxton
and his output in numbers was large, but his importance in the early history of English printing is
over-shadowed by that of Caxton. Both Caxton and
Wynken de Worde printed in Westminster, then a separate town but now a part of London, and the first
printer in old London proper was John Lettou, in 1480.
William de Machlinia, Richard Pynson, and Julian
Notary also printed in London before 1500, and other
presses were established in Oxford and St. Albans before the turn of the century. All were foreigners except Caxton and possibly the printer at St. Albans,
whose identity is unknown. On the whole, early English
printing is typographically undistinguished when compared to that produced in Europe during the same period. Caxton was apparently more interested in the literary quality of his publishing than in the physical perfection of the printing, and the other early English
printers, with the possible exception of Wynken de
Worde and Richard Pynson, seem to have been mere
journeyman printers, who never brought their trade to
perfection.

Considering the fact that there were very few printing presses in operation before 1475, the physical output of incunabula--books printed before 1500--is
nothing short of amazing. Taking into consideration the
fact that many printed works must have been lost, and
that more than 20,000 different works and editions have
survived, the total product of those primitive presses
proves the great need and demand that existed for the
printed word. Almost as amazing as the number is the
quality and variety of the printed matter. Practically
every extent piece of literature in the languages of
western Europe, or in Latin or Greek, plus many in
Hebrew, found its way into print in that prolific half-
century. There were nearly 500 editions of the Bible
and the Psalms, with several hundred more religious
works including Breviaries, Hymnals and Prayer-books.
With the various editions of the works of the Saints and
those of the early Christian philosophers, the grand
total of works of a religious nature formed about half
of the output of the fifteenth century presses. About ten

per cent of the incunabula were books of church or
civil law, including commentaries and text-books. Another twenty per cent or so were works of literature,
including both the classic and medieval writers, and
all the sciences put together made up not quite another
ten per cent. The remainder were divided between elementary text-books (mostly Latin grammars), histories
and travel.

Some of the authors and titles that enjoyed popularity
before 1500 might be of interest. They included, among
the Latin classics, the works of Cicero, Virgil, Ovid,
Seneca, Horace, Juvenal, Persius and Terence , in
roughly that order. In the Greek, there were the works
of Aristotle, Aristophanes, Aesop, Homer, Galen, Theo-
phrastus, Theocritus, and Euripides. Among the contemporary or nearly contemporary writers were
Petrarch and Dante, with the works of the former going through some forty editions. In history, the
Nuremburg Chronicle was one of the most important
books, but there were other similar contemporary
works. In the sciences there were volumes on agriculture, astronomy, mathematics, medicine and botany,
with many more on the pseudo-sciences like astrology
and alchemy. Several contemporary romances were
published, including an early best seller by Aeneas
Sylvius, entitled Concerning Two Lovers. Christopher
Columbus' Letter Concerning the Newly Discovered
Islands was a popular item in the 1490's, and went
through twelve editions, despite the fact that it was
only a four-page leaflet. Of English authors published
before 1500, perhaps the most significant was Geoffrey
Chaucer, whose Canterbury Tales were printed by Caxton.

All things considered, the art of printing made great
progress in its first half century. By 1500, the printed
book had reached its present form, with title page, illustrations, tables of contents, and even rudimentary
indexes. The printing press had reached a form that
was to be little changed for three hundred years, and
typography in general had reached a stage of near perfection, that has been improved upon only in the last
century. Though the making of books was still a laborious job, involving much hand work, it was far superior

to hand writing, and the literate world would no longer be handicapped through lack of reading material. The invention of the printing press brought about a cultural revolution, hardly surpassed by any other single development since the beginning of writing. Henceforth, man's ideas would have a ready vehicle for rapid and easy communication, so that a Martin Luther could begin a Reformation, and a Thomas Jefferson could start a Revolution--with a Declaration of Independence. Books, pamphlets and broadsides, journals, magazines and newspapers, all the products of the presses, were to play a major part in changing history. And the accumulation, preservation and distribution of this mass of printed material was to radically change the character of the library and the librarian.

Bibliography

Aldis, Harry G.: The printed book. Cambridge, England, 1951. 142 p.

Bennett, H.S.: English books and readers, 1475-1557. Cambridge, England, 1952. 336 p.

Bliss, Douglas P.: A history of wood-engraving. London, 1928. 256 p.

Blum, Andre: On the origin of paper. New York, 1934. 79 p.

------ The origins of printing and engraving. New York, 1940. 226 p.

Bullock, Warren B.: The romance of paper. Boston 1933. 88 p.

Butler, Pierce: The origin of printing in Europe. Chicago, 1940. 154 p.

Carter, Thomas F.: The invention of printing in China and its spread westward. New York, 1931. 282 p.

Clapperton, R.H.: Paper, an historical account of its making by hand from the earliest times down to the present day. Oxford, 1934. 158 p.

Davenport, Cyril: The book, its history and development. New York, 1930. 258 p.

Davies, Hugh W.: Devices of the early printers. London, 1935. 707 p.

DeVinne, T.L.: Notable printers of Italy during the fifteenth century. New York, 1910. 210 p.

Guppy, Henry: The beginnings of printed book illustration. Manchester, 1933. 45 p.

Hamilton, Frederick W.: A brief history of printing. Chicago, 1918. 2 vols.

Hess, Sol: Printing types: their origin and development. New York, 1947. 42 p.

Hind, Arthur M.: An introduction to a history of woodcut. New York, 1935. 2 vols.

Hunter, Dard: Paper making; the history and technique of an ancient craft. New York, 1947. 611 p.

Johnson, Henry L.: Gutenberg and the Book of books. New York, 1932. 24 p.

Laufer, Berthold: Paper and printing in ancient China. Chicago, 1931. 33 p.

McKerrow, Ronald B.: An introduction to bibliography for literary students. Oxford, 1927. 359 p. (See pp. 38-144)

McMurtrie, Douglas C.: The book; the story of printing and bookmaking. New York, 1943. 676 p. (McMurtrie has numerous pamphlets and books on special phases of the history of printing.)

Orcutt, William D.: The book in Italy during the fifteenth and sixteenth centuries. London, 1928. 220 p.

------ Master makers of the book. New York, 1928. 271 p.

Oswald, J.C.: A history of printing. New York, 1928. 403 p.

Peddie, Robert A.: Printing, a short history. London, 1927. 389 p.

Smith, A.M.: Printing and writing materials, their evolution. Philadelphia, 1901. 236 p.

Stillwell, Margaret B.: Incunabula and Americana. New York, 1931. 483 p.

Updike, Daniel B.: Printing types; their history, forms and use. Cambridge, Mass., 1946. 2 vols.

Von Hagen, Victor W.: The Aztec and Maya papermakers. New York, 1944. 120 p.

Wheelock, Mary E.: Paper, its history and development. Chicago, 1928. 12 p.

Winship, George P.: .Gutenberg to Plantin : outline of the early history of printing. Cambridge, Mass., 1926. 84 p.

------ John Gutenberg. Chicago, 1940. 38 p.

------ Printing in the fifteenth century. Philadelphia, 1940. 158 p.

Currier, C.W.: "Early labors of the printing-press,"
Catholic World, LXIII, (1896), 59-70.

Daniel, H.: "The Koreans were ahead of Gutenberg,"
Natural History, LX, (1951), 376-378.

Daland, Judson: "The evolution of modern printing and
the discovery of movable metal types by the Chinese
and Koreans in the fourteenth century," Journal of
the   Franklin Institute, CCXII, (1931), 209-234.

Jackson, Katherine: "The printer of the 15th century,"
South Atlantic Quarterly, VIII, (Oct. 1909), 361-369.

Keogh, Andrew: "The Gutenberg Bible as a typograph-
ical monument," Yale University Library Bulletin, I,
(1926), 1-6.

Prostov, Eugene V.: "Origins of Russian printing,"
Library Quarterly, I, (1931), 255-277.

Uhlendorff, G.A.: "The invention of printing and its
spread till 1470," Library Quarterly, II, (1932),
179-231.

V European Books and Libraries, 1500-1900

The total cultural effect of the invention of printing can hardly be over-estimated. The coming of printing meant that new ideas could be easily disseminated, could reach thousands of readers rather than a few score. It meant also that people could learn for the first time of Columbus and Copernicus, and of Plato and Aristotle. Learning, long shut up in monasteries and a few schools, emerged to become something that anyone with interest and initiative could pursue. Printing furthered the Renaissance that had already started, and facilitated the Reformation that soon followed. More books were being printed and more books were being read; more people were becoming educated and the Dark Ages were rapidly coming to an end. Probably more than any other single thing, the invention of printing ushered in the modern era.

The printing press changed the world of books. This change was achieved gradually over a period of half-century or more, as the products of the presses were increasing and filling the book-shelves of Europe. The bookseller ceased being a dealer in rare manuscripts alone, and could stock and sell the newly printed books in large numbers. Journeyman booksellers peddled their wares from town to town and from village to village. Later, with the publication of the cheaper chap-books, the chapman followed with his penny wares to sell to the poorest reader. In the publishing end of the book business, the new trades of printer, bookbinder, wood-cut artist, copper-plate engraver and bookseller added numbers to the rapidly growing middle class. In a few cases, the publishers became wealthy for the book business was, economically as well as culturally, a successful innovation.

In the library itself, the coming of the printed book brought many changes--but not at first. In fact, many librarians and book-collectors at first refused to have the new printed books in their libraries. In their eyes, the printed page was merely a poor imitation of the real thing. Gradually, however, the book replaced the manuscript rolls and codices, which became valuable rarities rather than objects of ordinary use. As books became more plentiful, they were placed on open shelves, rather than in chests or on lecterns. The library was separated from the scriptorium, and indeed, the latter disappeared, with many monasteries acquiring printing presses of their own instead. Printed books could be loaned for outside use, and thus public, circulating libraries became a possibility. The typical library became the oblong room with books around the wall, and with tables in the center for readers, or perhaps cases for displaying historical objects in place of the tables. The library room was open at stipulated times, and a librarian or keeper was on duty at those times. Various systems were used for arranging the books on the shelves, but in most cases, some system was employed and a catalog or finding list of the books was available. Finally, the sixteenth century library of printed books was larger than its medieval predecessor, and often numbered its contents in thousands of volumes. The modern library was still far from having arrived, but it was well on its way by 1600.

The books themselves in the sixteenth and seventeenth centuries varied widely in format and content. Many were still huge folios, resembling the bound volumes of manuscripts, but there were also the small popular books printed by Aldine in Italy, Elzevir in Holland, and others. In subject, religious works still lead in numbers, and the classics were still popular, but contemporary works ranging from science to superstition and from travel to romance were also widely published. The medieval wood-cut gave way after the middle of the sixteenth century to the copper-plate engraving, but not until after the wood-cut had reached a high stage of perfection under such artists as Hans Holbein and Albrecht Dürer. Book-bindings ranged from the paper back through the simple unlettered vellum to the highly ornate gold-embossed leathers. Printing types were changed, except in Germany, from the blackletter or Gothic types to lighter, more legible ones, and gradually the typeface ceased being a copy of contemporary handwriting and became an art form in its own right. In many respects, especially in France and the Low Countries, the printer's art reached a high point in the sixteenth and seventeenth centuries that was not surpassed and was rarely equalled in the eighteenth and nineteenth centuries.

Since the Renaissance had begun, more or less, in the Italian peninsula, and since the printing industry reached a high popularity there, it is only natural that Italian libraries also prospered in the fifteenth and sixteenth centuries. Several outstanding libraries were begun long before the printing press, but these were joined by others as books became more plentiful, and the profitable trade of Venice, Genoa and Naples produced merchant princes with funds to endow libraries. A few wealthy nobles, who had searched monastery libraries from Greece to England to purchase, purloin or copy writings for their collections, now added printed books to their libraries and opened them to the public or gave them to public institutions. The book treasures of the Medici family were opened to scholars in the Laurentian Library in Venice, and in that same city, the great library of St. Mark was housed in its own building in the 1540's. In 1609, the Biblioteca Ambrosiana, or Ambrosian Library, was opened to the public in Milan, largely through the efforts of the scholarly Archbishop of Milan, Federigo Borromeo. This library, which grew to contain many thousands of books, was open to any and all who wanted to come there to study, and had in connection with it a "College of Doctors", which was really a group of scholars engaged in continuous research. A printing press was provided to make available to all the results of their studies. Other Italian cities, such as Genoa, Rome and Naples, and smaller towns as well, had their libraries, public in the sense that they were free to all scholars. They were usually the gift of some merchant or nobleman, or else a collection brought together through the Church.

Of the Church collections, the most important was the Vatican Library in Rome, which, after many vicissitudes in the Middle Ages, began to grow rapidly in the sixteenth and seventeenth centuries. Many treasures from monastery libraries found their way to the Vatican as gifts to the various Popes, and occasionally whole libraries were added at once, as for instance in 1623 when Maximilian, Duke of Bavaria, took the Palatine Library of Heidelberg as spoils of war and gave it to Pope Gregory XV. In 1658, the Library of Urbino, founded by Duke Federigo some two centuries earlier, passed into the hands of the Pope, and was added to the Vatican Library. In 1588, Pope Sixtus V erected a magnificent building to house the Vatican Library, and greatly augmented the collection of books and manuscripts which it contained. Since the sixteenth century, the course of the papal library has been upward, except for a brief set-back early in the nineteenth century, when the French under Napoleon took a few of its treasures, only to return them after that Emperor's fall from power. The Vatican librarians have been generally of very high quality, numbering among them several outstanding writers and historians, such as the seventeenth century church historian, Baronius. Other Vatican librarians began the task of cataloging the valuable contents, and took steps to preserve the thousands of manuscripts already centuries old. Printed books were separated from the manuscripts, and among the latter the codices were separated from the rolls, and the Greek, Latin and Hebrew works were divided. Some of the more important manuscripts were enshrined in separate cases. By the end of the nineteenth century, the Vatican Library was easily one of the most important in the world. It contained over 400,000 printed books, with 4,000 incunabula; more than 30,000 Latin, over 4,000 Greek and also more than 3,000 Oriental manuscripts, with the latter division including the Hebrew. So important has the Vatican Library been considered in the history of the Catholic Church that many of its most important leaders have been honored with the post of chief librarian, and several of these have been promoted, in time, to the position of Pope.

The libraries in France after 1500 owed much to Italian precedents, just as did its medieval libraries. The French tended to improve or broaden the Italian beginnings, and promoted a professional librarianship

61

that was hardly realized in Italy. France had the advantage over Italy of being a unified nation, at least after the 16th century, and this gave rise to a French national library, the Bibliothèque Nationale. The Bibliothèque Nationale had its beginnings in several royal libraries, but the national library as such is usually dated from Francis I (1494-1547). In 1538, that monarch strengthened the national book collection by ordering that one copy of each book printed in France should be donated to it, but unfortunately neither that order, nor another issued in 1617, raising the required number to two copies, was strictly enforced. The philologist, Guillaume Budé, was one of the first librarians of the Bibliotheque Nationale, and he is generally considered responsible for the first organization of the collection into library form. In the early seventeenth century, several important private collections of books and manuscripts were added to the national library, including the library of Catherine de Medici, queen of Henry II and a literary figure in her own right. By 1622, the library had its first printed catalog, which listed some 6,000 volumes, mostly manuscripts, but so rapidly did it grow that by the end of that century it contained more than 70,000 volumes. Its growth was considerably enhanced during the Napoleonic period through volumes seized in the conquest of other countries, but most of these were later returned. By 1900, the Bibliotheque Nationale was one of the major libraries of the world, with more than three million books, maps, manuscripts and prints.

An early rival of the French national library was the Bibliothèque Mazarine, founded by Cardinal Mazarin under the direction of the librarian, Gabriel Naudé. Naudé (1600-1653) had book agents search all over Europe for books and manuscripts to add to the Cardinal's library, and by 1650 it contained some 40,000 volumes, mostly richly bound in leather and stamped with the Cardinal's seal. This library was open to the public, or at least to those students who had the Cardinal's favor. Naudé, in addition to cataloging and arranging the Mazarin library, also wrote one of the earliest books on library science. This was his Avis pour Dresser une Bibliothèque, or Advice on Establishing a Library, published in 1627. In this work Naudé proclaimed the necessity for having all types of books in a library, new and old, rare and common, religious and profane. He recommended a system of classification based on the faculties, or branches of knowledge usually taught in the universities, but he subdivided these into smaller classes for convenience. He hoped the Bibliothèque Mazarine would become a universal library, preserving the literary heritage of all peoples, and he set out to make it so. Unfortunately, the library was virtually destroyed in the 1650's by Mazarin's political enemies, only to be reconstituted a decade later. As the library of the College de Mazarine it has continued as one of the great reference libraries of Paris.

Elsewhere in France, most of the notable libraries of the sixteenth to nineteenth centuries were either those of the universities or of the nobles. Some of the towns developed public libraries at an early date, such as the Bibliothèque Municipale of Troyes, founded in 1651, but these were more in the nature of museums than libraries. Some of the monastery libraries underwent transformations and emerged as university or other institutional libraries, and a good example of this is the Bibliothèque Ste. Genevieve, in Paris, which began as the library of the Abbey of Ste. Genevieve, and grew until by the twentieth century it was a national reference library of over 400,000 volumes. During the French Revolution, many religious libraries, both monastic and cathedral, were confiscated by the state, and since that period most of the library development has been on a national basis, except for a few private universities and endowed institutional libraries. Reference libraries were fairly numerous in France, particularly in Paris and the larger cities in the eighteenth and nineteenth centuries, but public library service as we know it in America today was virtually unknown before 1900.

In Germany, there was no national unity until the nineteenth century, so each German state developed its own library, and many of them were deservedly famous. Prussia, the largest German state, had its State Library in Berlin, founded by Frederick William, the Great Elector, in 1661. Before his death he had built this collection to more than 20,000 volumes and 1500 manuscripts, all cataloged and classified according to the system advocated by Naudé. Earlier Prussian princes had set up at Konigsberg the so-called "Silver Library," where the ornate bindings were tooled in silver. Duke Albrecht V (1550-1579) founded the State Library of Bavaria at Munich with his own private library as its nucleus. It was housed in a separate building in 1575, and contained over 20,000 volumes by 1600. Julius, Duke of Brunswick, founded the Duke's Library at Wolfenbüttel in 1558, and this collection by the eighteenth century, when the dramatist Gotthold Ephraim Lessing was its librarian, numbered over 60,000 volumes. The other German states and principalities also had libraries, usually founded by the nobility, by the eighteenth century, and most of them grew into considerable size by the nineteenth. Their holdings also included many valuable early printed works and manuscripts, making them important research collections.

In competition with the princes, wealthy German merchants also created and endowed libraries. Ulrich Fugger, wealthy merchant and bibliophile, helped found the Palatine library at Heidelberg, which ended up as spoils of war in the Vatican Library. Many other European libraries, even as late as the nineteenth century, became involved in military conquests and changed hands and countries, sometimes more than once.

Besides the private libraries, at least three other major types arose in Germany in the sixteenth and seventeenth centuries. These were the church libraries, the municipal libraries, and the university libraries. During the Reformation many of the monastery libraries in Germany were closed and their contents wound up in some of the other libraries, usually the princely collections. In place of the monastery library, however, came the church library. Martin Luther taught that everyone should read the Bible and he translated it into German so that it could be read. He encouraged the Lutheran churches to provide books for the people to read, and so popular libraries came to be connected with the village church in most cases. These were quite different from the old monastery collections, and were apparently well used, even though their contents were almost entirely religious. Another type of popular library was the municipal or "alderman's" library. One of these was founded at Nuremberg in 1445, but most of them date from later centuries. In the larger cities these grew into very large reference collections, but in the smaller towns they usually remained rather small, even though their use might be considerable. The German university libraries were also notable for their size and contents. At Jena, Leipzig, Heidelberg and Konigsberg, to mention only a few of the more prominent universities, there developed during the sixteenth and seventeenth centuries scholarly libraries far superior to those in other European countries. By the nineteenth century many of these collections numbered their volumes in the hundreds of thousands, with some approaching a half million. Not only were these collections large and important from the research point of view, but they were well organized and manned by scholar-librarians who operated them according to definite library procedures.

Among these early German librarians was Gottfried Wilhelm Leibniz, who, after working some years in the French Bibliothèque Nationale, returned to Hanover to become librarian of the Royal Library there in 1676. At Hanover, Leibniz created an alphabetical catalog for the library, and also directed the construction of one of the earliest library buildings. Besides his practical accomplishments, Leibniz is remembered for his writings about the place of the library in society, and his general philosophy of librarianship. He recommended continued financial support of libraries by their patrons or the state, and saw the public library as both a popular reading collection and a research center. He deplored those who judged a library by its numbers, or by its bindings, and said that the only true evaluation of a library was by the quality of the books in it. In addition to his alphabetical catalog of authors, he recommended a subject catalog or index, and also a chronological index by date of publication. Many of Leibniz' ideas about library service were more fully realized in the German libraries of the next century.

An outstanding German librarian of the nineteenth

century was Fritz Ebert, head of the Wolfenbüttel Library. In his book on the training of the librarian, Ebert was rather critical of the average library of his day. In particular, he found the usual university library to be poorly organized, in charge of inexpert personnel, and filled with treasures that were all but lost for the average scholar who used the library. He was a little more charitable to the municipal libraries, but these too he felt had suffered from maladministration and untrained workers. He urged that librarianship be raised to the status of a full-time, trained profession, but unfortunately few people agreed with him at that time.

All things considered, though, the German libraries of the nineteenth century were probably the best in the world. The variety in kinds of libraries, the numbers of all types, the size of the major ones, the professional interest and ability of the librarians, and the financial backing afforded by church, state and wealthy patrons, all combined to make this possible. By the early nineteenth century, German librarians were already familiar with such library developments as circulating libraries, popular reading rooms, published bibliographies and catalogs, inter-library loans, and even union catalogs. By 1900, all types of libraries, even children's collections, were fairly common in Germany, and most of them were well used. As an example, there were in that year 268 libraries in Berlin alone, containing all together more than 5,000,000 volumes. In Munich, a much smaller city, there were 46 libraries, with more than 2,000,000 volumes and 60,000 important manuscripts.

In other parts of Europe libraries progressed in varying degrees after the coming of printing, with the west and north of Europe in general being far ahead of the east and southeast. In Austria, the Royal Library at Vienna was founded in 1440 by Emperor Frederick III. It grew slowly with some additions under the emperors Maximilian I and Ferdinand I, and by 1600 it had only about 1500 manuscripts and 10,000 printed books. One of its early librarians was Enea Silvio Piccolomini, who later became Pope Pius II. In the nineteenth century the Austrian Royal Library grew more rapidly, especial-

ly after a royal decree ordered that one copy of each
book printed in Austria-Hungary should be deposited
there. By 1900 it contained over a million volumes, a-
long with an important manuscript collection, and one
of the largest groups of Egyptian papyri in existence.
Other important libraries in Austria were the Innsbruck
University library, founded in 1746, and that of the University of Vienna, which dates from 1775.

In Belgium, the Royal Library at Brussels was founded in 1837, but it was based on the library of the Dukes
of Burgundy, dating back to the fifteenth century. The
municipal library at Antwerp was founded in the sixteenth century, and is one of the oldest continuously
operating public libraries in Europe. There were important university libraries at Ghent and Louvain, and
large municipal libraries at Brussels and Liege. In
the nineteenth century, public libraries were established
in most of the Belgian towns, with varying degrees of
success. In the Netherlands, the Royal Library was
formed in 1798, on the basis of the library of the
Princes of Orange and several smaller collections. In
1900 it contained over a half million volumes. The
University of Utrecht library was begun in 1636, but
many of its books came from a municipal collection
gathered by the town fathers nearly a century earlier.
The University of Leiden was virtually built around a
library donated by the first William of Orange in 1575,
and the University of Amsterdam library grew out of a
church collection dating back to the fifteenth century.
Some of the older and more important libraries in the
Scandinavian countries are: The University of Copenhagen Library, founded in 1482; the Royal Library of
Denmark, 1539; the Free Public Library of Oslo, 1780;
the University of Oslo Library, 1811; the Royal Library
of Sweden, 1585; and that of the University of Uppsala,
perhaps the oldest library in Sweden, founded in 1477
and greatly enlarged by Gustavus Adolphus in 1620. In
all the Scandinavian countries the movement toward
popular libraries and reading rooms in all towns and
provinces became particularly strong after about 1850.

In Spain and Portugal, the private libraries of the
medieval scholars declined after the Moslems were
driven out in the fifteenth century, and although the

monasteries and the Church developed libraries there afterward, they did not compare with those of France or Germany. The National Library at Madrid was founded by Philip V in 1711, and became the most important library in Spain in size and quality of collection. Also in Madrid, the Central University Library, founded in 1508, is noted for its collections on Spanish history and literature. The National Library of Portugal, founded at Lisbon in 1786, is the most valuable library in that country, although the Municipal Library at Oporto almost equalled it in size in the nineteenth century. Several universities in Spain and Portugal had notable collections of books and manuscripts, including those at Seville, Barcelona, Salamanca and Coimbra. Many private libraries in these countries reached considerable size for such collections in the eighteenth and nineteenth centuries, but interest in public and college libraries lagged considerably behind that in the other areas of western Europe.

In Russia the greater libraries date for the most part from the eighteenth century, and several of them had their beginnings in libraries taken in wars with neighboring countries. The Imperial Library in St. Petersburg (Leningrad) began with the seizure of several libraries in Latvia in 1714, and it was enlarged considerably in 1796 with the capture of thousands of books and manuscripts from Poland. In the nineteenth century it was enlarged through the legal deposit of two copies of each book printed in Russia, and through the acquisition of many entire collections of books, usually donated by merchants or nobles. By 1900 it was one of the largest libraries in the world, with some 2,000,000 volumes. Other large libraries in Russia before 1900 included the Academy Library at St. Petersburg, founded in 1725; the Goruyi Institute Library there (1773); the University of Moscow Library (1755); and the Public Library at Moscow, which dates from 1689. Other large Russian cities began municipal libraries in the nineteenth centuries, such as Kharkov in 1886, and Odessa, in 1830. The University of Helsingfors (Helsinki) in Finland, began its library in 1640, while that of Cracow, Poland, goes back to 1400 or earlier. Elsewhere in eastern Europe, libraries, whether public or private, religious or educational, were far behind those in the western countries, at least down to 1900. The same was true in the Balkan states, where Turkish domination or influence lasted well into the nineteenth century. There were a few scholarly libraries, scattered and small, but nothing to resemble the collections in western Europe.

Along with the development of libraries, the invention of printing spurred on several other developments in the literary world, including particularly the publishing of periodicals and encyclopedias. The periodical began with the pamphlet in the sixteenth century, developed into a sporadic series of related pamphlets, into annual or biennial "registers" of the news, and finally, by the seventeenth century, into the regular periodical. Newspapers, largely weekly or bi-weekly, developed in much the same way from the broadside in the late seventeenth century and became fairly common a half-century later. Newspapers and periodicals together widened the impact of the printed word, and introduced new sources of income for the ambitious printer. The encyclopedias, created by almost a school of writers in the seventeenth century, were an outgrowth of many medieval attempts at collecting all available knowledge into one book or set of books. In 1630, Johann Heinrich Alsted published in Switzerland what was probably the first modern encyclopedia. He arranged his reference book topically, under seven major heads with some thirty-five subdivisions. Later in that century, two Frenchmen, Pierre Bayle and Louis Moreri, both produced encyclopedias, with that of Bayle being usually considered the most accurate and informative. In 1729, Ephraim Chambers published his two-volume Cyclopedia in English, with the subtitle, An Universal Dictionary of Arts and Sciences. This was later translated into French, and from it, with considerable revision and addition there came the famous Encyclopédie of Denis Diderot, which appeared between 1751 and 1780 in thirty volumes. By the end of the eighteenth century, the encyclopedia had reached virtually its modern form, complete with illustrations, long articles by many authorities, alphabetic arrangement, and cross references.

Generally speaking, the sixteenth and seventeenth centuries brought the art of printing to a stage of perfection that it did not surpass in the eighteenth and nineteenth. The whole era from 1500 to 1900 saw only slow progress in the book world, but that progress accelerated in the nineteenth century as a part of the general industrial revolution. In the library field, much the same is true. After the library had adapted itself to the changes brought on by printing, there was relatively little improvement in functions or services. and not much more in the numbers of libraries or in their size. Germany in the eighteenth and nineteenth century stands out as a library center for Europe, just as Italy did in the fifteenth and sixteenth. By the nineteenth century the growth of democratic ideas and the improved economic conditions of the middle class gave force to a movement throughout most of western Europe for popular libraries.

Bibliography

Andreae, George: The dawn of juvenile literature in England. Amsterdam, 1925. 122 p.

Cotton des Houssayes, Jean Baptiste: Duties and qualifications of a librarian. (1780). Chicago, 1906. 56 p.

Ebert, Friederich A.: The training of a librarian. (1820). Woodstock, Vermont, 1916. 39 p.

Edwards, Edward: A statistical view of the principal libraries of Europe and America. London, 1849. 48 p.

------ Libraries and founders of libraries. London, 1864. 503 p.

------ Memoirs of libraries. London, 1859. 2 v.

Hessel, Alfred: A history of libraries. New Brunswick 1955. 198 p.

Johnson, Alfred F.: French sixteenth century printing. London, 1928. 32 p.

Lipsius, Justus: A brief outline of the history of libraries. Chicago, 1907. 121 p.

Koch, Theodore W.: The Imperial Public Library at St. Petersburg, New York, 1915. 35 p.

Krieger, Bogdan: Frederick the Great and his books. New York, 1913. 24 p.

Mumby, Frank A: Publishing and bookselling, a history. New York, 1954.

Naudé, Gabriel: Advice on establishing a library (1650). Berkeley, Calif., 1950. 110 p.

Norris, Dorothy M,: A history of cataloging and cataloging methods, 1100-1850. London, 1939 246 p.

Orcutt, W.D.: The magic of the book. Boston, 1930.
315 p. (See pp. 63-104.)

------ Master makers of the book. New York, 1928.
271 p.

Pollard, Alfred W.: Early illustrated books. London,
1917. 256 p.

------ Fine books. London, 1912. 331 p.

Rice, James: Gabriel Naudé. Baltimore, 1939. 134 p.

Savage, Ernest A.: The story of libraries and book
collecting. New York, 1909. 230 p.

Tisserant, Eugene: The Vatican Library. Jersey City,
N.J., 1929. 31 p.

Encyclopedia Americana, (1929), v. 17, pp.357-378.

Encyclopedia Britannica, 11th ed., v. 16, pp. 548-577.

Garnett, Ricard: "Librarianship in the 17th century,"
in pp. 174-190 of his Essays in Librarianship and
Bibliography. London, 1899.

Gosnell, Charles F.: "Goethe the librarian," Library
Quarterly, II, (1932), 367-374.

Maass, Ernest: "Leibniz' contributions to librarianship,"College and Research Libraries, IV, (1943),
245-249.

Munthe, Wilhelm: "The library history of Norway,"
Library Journal, XLV, (1921), 19-24, 57-62.

Rostenberg, Leona: "The libraries of three Nuremberg
patricians, 1491-1568." Library Quarterly, XIII,
(1943), 21-33.

------ "The library of Johann Albrecht, Duke of
Mecklenburg, 1526-1576," Library Quarterly, XV,
(1945), 131-138.

Trenkler, Ernst: "History of the Austrian National-
bibliothek," Library Quarterly, XVII, (1947), 224-231.

VI English Books and Libraries, 1500-1900

English libraries, for the most part, developed like those on the continent, at least down to the fifteenth century. There were the early monastery libraries, and also the beginning of the university libraries. After about 1500, however, English library history began to develop in a manner of its own.

Both the book arts and libraries in England was severely retarded in the 1530's by the "burning of the books", which followed the Act of Dissolution, separating the Church of England from the Catholic Church. The property of the church was transferred to the King, and in the process, many monastery libraries were broken up and their contents sold or destroyed. The cathedral libraries at York and Canterbury managed to escape much of this damage, but there and in many other libraries as well, all books that were considered pro-Catholic were purged. The printing trade was heavily censored, and nothing could be printed without the approval of the government. When this literary purge was over, the Cambridge University library was reported to contain only 180 volumes, and it had saved only nineteen manuscripts out of 600 which it had possessed. The accession of Queen Elizabeth I in 1558 brought an end to this tragic period, but not until after many literary treasures had been lost, and library development in England had received a costly setback.

The Elizabethan period saw something of a revival in the English literary world, and also a period of progress in libraries. The Oxford University library, for example, was greatly enlarged and strengthened through the activities of Sir Thomas Bodley. Bodley, having achieved success in business and diplomacy, retired in 1587 and devoted himself to building up the collection at Oxford. So effective were his efforts that in later years the library there took his name, and to this day it is known as the Bodleian Library. By 1602, Bodley had built the Oxford Library to about 2,000 volumes. In 1613, it had grown so that an annex was needed, and by 1620, the first regular librarian, Thomas James, could report that the library contained 16,000 volumes. Many important accessions came later, including 1,300 manuscripts donated by Archbishop Laud in 1646, and by 1700, the Oxford Library was the largest and most important in England.

The Cambridge University Library did not fare as well in the seventeenth century as did the Bodleian, but it did grow slowly, and on several occasions received aid from the Royal or Commonwealth government. One important collection added was a large group of Arabic manuscripts from the library of Thomas Erpenius of Leiden. During the Civil War and Commonwealth period, 1641-1660, the fortunes of the Cambridge library varied, sometimes losing, sometimes gaining a few volumes. After the Restoration of King Charles II, however, it received some royal attention, and in addition, in 1666, it received from Bishop Tobias Rustat, an endowment of ₤1000 which returned a small annual income. In addition to the university libraries, many of the individual colleges at the universities also possessed libraries of considerable size and value. In many cases, these college libraries had endowments in their own right, and were better off financially than the university collections. The college library collections were usually more restricted in scope and use was usually limited to the students of the particular college.

In addition to Oxford and Cambridge, the University of Glasgow Library, founded in 1453, was an important educational asset in the sixteenth and seventeenth centuries. The University of St. Andrews in Scotland is known to have had a library as early as 1456, but its organization as a university collection dates from 1610. Edinburgh University Library was founded in 1583, largely on a gift of funds and books from Clement Little, a wealthy merchant-lawyer. A fourth Scottish university library, at Aberdeen, was in operation by 1634, but it never equalled the others in importance. In Ireland, the library of Trinity College in Dublin was

73

begun with a gift of books by the English army after a victory over the Irish at the battle of Kinsale in 1601. By 1604, this collection had 4,000 volumes, and it grew steadily after that to become the most important library in Ireland. James Usher, later primate of Ireland, directed the early growth of the collection, and on his death in 1655, willed his own library of 7,000 volumes and 600 manuscripts to it.

In the eighteenth and nineteenth centuries, the story of English university libraries was one of slow progress. In many cases the college libraries merged with those of the universities, but others retained their identity. Important gifts were added to the collections, especially at Oxford and Cambridge, as in 1715 when George I presented the library of the latter institution with a gift of over 30,000 volumes. Cambridge moved its library into a new building in 1755, and Oxford University Library, after several other moves, went into the new Radcliffe Camera building in 1860. By 1900, both institutions had libraries of over half million volumes. Elsewhere in England and Scotland, many new colleges and universities emerged in the nineteenth century particularly, and each of these built up imposing libraries. Some of these were the University of London, (1837); University of Durham, (1832); Victoria University at Manchester, (1851); and the University of Liverpool (1882).

The national library of England, the British Museum, has had a long and interesting history. The early rulers of England had acquired collections of books, particularly Queen Elizabeth I, whose library was noted for the beauty of its bindings. In 1570, Sir Humphrey Gilbert, a favorite of Elizabeth's, drew up a plan for a Royal Academy and Library, and similar ideas were advanced by Roger Ascham, who was the Royal librarian. Neither of these plans was successful, however, and the Royal library remained simply a private collection. Throughout the troubled Civil War and Commonwealth period following the execution of Charles I, the Royal Library was kept intact, largely through the efforts of its librarian at that time, John Dury. Dury took his position seriously, and even published a booklet, entitled The Reformed Librarie Keeper, which contained some surprisingly modern ideas. The librarian was pictured by Dury as the main figure in the process of learning, the chief factor in bringing the book and the reader together. One of his successors, Richard Bentley, who became Royal librarian in 1694, made the King's collection a semi-public one, and wrote a pamphlet on A Proposal for Building a Royal Library and Establishing It by Act of Parliament. He wanted governmental aid to build the library to the size of at least 200,000 volumes, and to support it permanently as a public institution. His plan was good, but premature, and it was not until a half-century later that a similar plan was put into effect.

Sir Hans Sloane, a physician and scientist, is the man most directly responsible for the founding of the British Museum. During his life he collected books and manuscripts, and also museum pieces from antique furniture to botanical specimens. On his death, he willed his collection to the nation on condition that it be suitably housed and displayed to the public. In 1753, Parliament accepted this offer, and united the Sloane Collection with two others, the Cottonian and Harleian Libraries, to form the beginnings of the British Museum, which was finally opened to the public in 1759. The Cottonian was largely the collection of Sir Robert Bruce Cotton, whose grandson donated the library to the government. The Harley Library was purchased by Parliament from the heirs of Sir Robert Harley, who had collected it early in the eighteenth century. This collection was largely manuscripts, and formed the foundation upon which the outstanding manuscript library of the British Museum was later built. King George II donated his private library, including the remains of several previous Royal libraries, to the Museum before his death in 1760. George III, who reigned from 1760 to 1820, collected a library reputed to total over 100,000 volumes. Many of these books were later added to the British Museum, as were also many of the manuscript and art treasures which this royal bibliophile amassed.

Although the British Museum was the national library, it was still a museum, and its main purpose was to display the curios and rarities collected over the years by the various donors. Hence, Montagu House in London, the first home of the Museum, was largely a show place for the scientific collection, and the books were shelved in rooms off the main display hall. The first three librarians were all scientists, and the book and manuscript collections did not receive the attention which they merited until well into the nineteenth century. The librarian who was to transform the Museum into one of the greatest libraries in the world was, oddly enough, not even an Englishman. He was Anthony Panizzi, an Italian political refugee, who in 1831 became an assistant librarian in the Museum thanks to a friendship he had formed with a member of the Board of Trustees. He knew little of library work before his appointment, but he was well learned in European languages and literatures, and he became expert in bibliography as well. Although he was Head Librarian only from 1856 to 1866, his entire thirty-five years on the staff were spent in improving the book and manuscript collection, and in making it more useful to the public. He has been called the second founder of the Museum library. He pointed up the weaknesses in the collection, and urged larger appropriations to fill in the gaps. He insisted on enforcing the deposit laws which required publishers to supply the library with all British publications. When he joined the staff the Museum library was the seventh largest in Europe, but when he resigned it was second only to the French Bibliothèque Nationale. But probably more than anything else, Panizzi is remembered for designing the circular reading room which was opened to the public in 1857. It was said of Panizzi that he took a book collection and made a library out of it, and it might be added that in doing that he made of himself one of the world's greatest librarians. By 1900, the British Museum contained over 2,000,000 volumes, along with nearly 5,000,000 additional items including pamphlets, manuscripts, prints, pictures and museum objects.

The private collection has played a major role, in English library history, particularly since the seventeenth century. In so many cases these private libraries later became a primary part of, or substantial additions to important public and college collections. A few examples of the more notable private collections,

many of them gathered by several generations of a
noble family, will serve to indicate their importance.
The Earls of Balcarres developed the Biblioteca
Lindesiana, of which the most valuable parts eventually were given to the John Rylands Library in Manchester. The Dukes of Marlborough developed at Blenheim
a library which by the early nineteenth century
numbered over 20,000 volumes. Lord Fitzwilliam bequeathed his library of works on science and art to
Cambridge University in 1816. But the nobles were
not the only Englishmen to acquire libraries. John
Selden, a lawyer, who died in 1654, willed a collection
of more than 8,000 volumes to the Bodleian Library,
while the historian, William Camden, left a large library at his death in 1623, and this collection eventually
ended up in the British Museum. In 1678, the Reverend James Nairne gave, 2,000 books to the University
of Edinburgh Library. And so the story goes--book
collectors competing with each other to acquire books
and manuscripts, and then in the end willing, donating
or selling their libraries to some institution. Not all
of the great English private libraries came into public
hands, of course, and not all of them remained in
England. Some were acquired by American buyers and
eventually became parts of libraries on this side of the
Atlantic, while others went to French and German collectors.

Professional libraries were notable by the eighteenth
century. Lincoln's Inn, a legal corporation that was
noted as a training school for lawyers, had a professional library dating from 1508. Gray's Inn and the
Inner Temple, similar legal organizations, had large
libraries in the eighteenth century, and the latter was
open to the public as well as to its own lawyers. The
Royal Society, a scholarly scientific organization had an
important library from its founding in 1667. It specialized in transactions and publications of learned societies all over the world, and by the nineteenth century
numbered over 75,000 volumes. In Edinburgh, the Sig-
net (law) Library was founded in 1722, and in the other
larger cities legal, religious and scientific professional
libraries were common by the nineteenth century. They
were particularly numerous in London, including large
collections in medicine, natural history, archaeology,

geology, geography, chemistry, botany, zoology and the fine arts.

There were several attempts to provide books for the average reader, but it was not until the late nineteenth century that much was accomplished. A public library was established in Coventry in 1601, but it did not survive. One established in Manchester in 1654 has survived almost intact, indicating that it was little used. The library in Dundee, Scotland, dates from 1601, and that of Bristol, England, from 1613, but there is some doubt as to the public character of these institutions in their early centuries. They were indeed public property, but the book collections were small, the caretakers were often indifferent, and the amount of public use is questionable. Probably of more use were the parish libraries founded by Reverend Thomas Bray and his associates around 1700. These libraries were for the use of ministers and church members, and were mostly religious in nature, but they apparently had wide popularity during Bray's lifetime. In later years those that survived tended to become merely ministerial collections, and as such more professional in nature than public.

During the latter half of the eighteenth century two other types of semi-public libraries became fairly common in England. These were the proprietary and subscription libraries. The former were usually connected with some organization and operated on a nonprofit basis, while the latter were commercial. An example of the proprietary type was the mechanics' library, which was designed to provide educational and recreational reading matter for apprentices or workers in particular locations or trades. Others were formed by co-operative societies, working-men's clubs, and trade unions, and many of them eventually formed the bases of local public libraries. They usually included trade manuals, textbooks, religious and political pamphlets, and occasionally more serious literary and historical works. They were usually open only to members. The subscription library, on the other hand, was open to any one who could pay the fee. These were more in the nature of book clubs or rental book services, and may have had their origin in the coffee-house libraries of the seventeenth century. Around the universities and in the larger towns, the more popular inns or coffee-houses kept book collections for their patrons. These books could be read on the premises, or borrowed for a small sum. Regular patrons paid an annual rental for the use of the books, and in at least one case this rate was only one shilling for a year. The popularity of these collections stemmed from their contents: political pamphlets, poems and plays that were available nowhere else except by purchase. Needless to say, the early book publishers complained of this service, arguing that it was depriving them of sales. The subscription library as it developed in the late eighteenth century was patterned on this idea, but was usually formed around a printing house or book store, enjoyed a more permanent membership, and carried books of a more scholarly nature. The subscription library was a popular means of obtaining reading matter, patronized by scholar and noble alike, along with many a poorer printer and tradesman. Together with the proprietary libraries, they formed the real public libraries of the era before 1850.

The subjects closely connected with books and libraries are the copyright and legal deposit. The first refers to the author's or publisher's legal rights to a published work, and the latter to the legal requirement that one or more copies of all published works be deposited in certain designated libraries. In 1556, the Stationers' Company was incorporated in London as an association of printers and publishers representing all such tradesmen in England. In effect it was a monopoly of the publishing business, because non-members were unable to get government permits for operation. Previous to 1556, what amounted to a copyright to a published work could be secured by obtaining a "privilege" from the King for printing a book. In later years, the entry of a book title in the register of the Stationers' Company gave the publisher exclusive rights to his publication for an indefinite term. In 1661, the first Licensing Act replaced the Stationers' register with a copyright law, which, with many revisions has continued in operation to the present. Legal deposit originated in 1610, when Sir Thomas Bodley induced the Stationers' Company to place one copy of each book published by their members in the library of Oxford University. This practice was made legal and permanent in the Licensing Act, and two other libraries, that at Cambridge University and the Royal Library in London, were added to the deposit list. In the eighteenth century, legal deposit was extended to other English, Scottish and Irish libraries, but during the nineteenth century the number of depository libraries was curtailed considerably. It had been found that the deposit laws were being consistently evaded, and when a stronger copyright law was passed in 1852, deposit was required only for the British Museum, while four other major libraries could obtain free depository copies by requesting them in writing.

The development of the modern English public library began in the middle of the nineteenth century. In 1847, following numerous requests from churchmen, social reformers, and trade union leaders, Parliament passed an act appointing a Committee on Public Libraries to consider the necessity of establishing them throughout the nation. Two years later this Committee presented a very full report on the condition of library service then available in England, and the need for a tax-supported free public library service. In 1850, as a result of this report, the Public Libraries Act was passed, allowing cities of 10,000 or more population to levy taxes to support library service. Subsequent laws of 1870 and 1876 made such taxes available for smaller towns and rural areas, and by 1877 seventy-seven cities had formed public libraries. By 1900, the number of public libraries had passed 300 and many of the larger ones had branches. However, except in the larger cities, public library service was poorly supported in England before World War I, and there was little in the way of library extension for rural areas. As it happened, the growth of the public library movement came at a time when many of the great private libraries of England were being broken up, and some of their most valuable books and manuscripts found their way into the public libraries, so that today many British municipal libraries have important research and rare book collections.

England saw little progress in printing in the sixteenth and seventeenth centuries. After a good beginning under Caxton and his fellow printers of the late fifteenth century, English printing felt the burden of censorship and unsettled economic and political conditions. Printers were plentiful, but their output was closely watched by both government and religious censors, and it was not until after the Restoration of the Stuart kings in 1660 that much progress was made in either quantity or quality of printing. Typography was a trade and not an art in England, and even the printing of the Shakespearean plays was poorly done. The types used were often old and worn, margins were small, title-pages were poorly designed, and illustrations were often so carelessly printed as to be hardly recognizable. A few fine books were printed, such as Thomas Roycroft's Polyglot Bible of 1657, and a few books from the press at Oxford University, but for almost two centuries the English printing trade was at a low level. This picture changed in the eighteenth century, however, and at that time England's printing was among the best in Europe. William Caslon began, about 1720, to develop new type-faces, taking his patterns from the better Dutch printers and improving upon them. His type was clean and clear, and he used a combination of curves and angles in his letters that was pleasing to the eye. John Baskerville, in turn, took the Caslon type-forms, adapted them moderately, and with them produced some of the most beautiful books in printing history. Baskerville improved upon the type he used and upon the press, paper and ink as well. He printed some sixty-seven different books, but probably his best known book is his edition of the works of Virgil. Baskerville's books were expensive, even for his day, and they were designed mostly for the collector, but they set a standard of perfection and even elegance in printing that has influenced the book world ever since.

The output of the English printers, at first, was religious works, political pamphlets, and the classical authors, although the latter were never printed as freely in England as they were upon the continent. In the sixteenth century, however, there was more pamphleteering, more works by English authors, and government publications. In the seventeenth century came the King James Bible, which was published in several large editions, and the first periodicals. These were usually folded sheets of four or eight pages, and gave the most recent political or military news, along with the editor's personal opinions on such matters. Usually these early journals were short-lived, unless they enjoyed political or government support, and their fortunes varied with the political prestige of their editors. In the eighteenth century, the periodical came into its own, with newspapers, magazines, and yearbooks fairly common and important, both from a political and a literary point of view. There were general and news magazines, such as the Gentleman's Magazine, literary periodicals, such as the Spectator, and important yearbooks, like the Annual Register. Scientific books and journals joined the literary output of the English presses in the late eighteenth and nineteenth centuries, and, in general, the press of England became and remained as free and prolific as any in the world.

Although they were not printed in large numbers before 1900 there were a few children's books published. In 1477 Caxton published his Boke of Curteseye, or book of manners for young people, to instruct the young Englishman on how to act in church, and at home, and, oddly enough, on what to read. The Schoole of Vertue and Book of Good Nurture for Children and Youth to Learn Their Duty By was a similar work, written by F.S. Seager and printed in 1577. About 1600 there appeared the horn book, the first elementary reading book designed for the child's own use. The horn book was really a single printed page, fastened to a wooden paddle, and protected by a transparent cover of horn. The World in Pictures, first printed in England in 1658 has been considered the first picture book for children. About the middle of the eighteenth century, John Newbery became one of the first publishers to be particularly interested in children's books. He published a collection of Mother Goose Rhymes and Oliver Goldsmith's History of Margery Two-Shoes, which is considered to be the first story in English written especially for children. In all, Newbery published more than a hundred small books for his juvenile readers, and was himself the author of many of them. He was also one of the first publishers of annual gift-books, which were to become so popular in the nineteenth century.

One other publishing development of the eighteenth

century is worthy of note. This was the compiling and publishing of multi-volumed encyclopedias. One of the first of these was Ephraim Chambers' Cyclopedia, or Universal Dictionary of Arts and Sciences, published in 1728. This was a two volume work, and is notable for being arranged in alphabetic order, and for introducing the cross reference, or at least making good use of it for the first time in a major English reference work. Chambers' encyclopedia was followed in 1771 by the first edition of the Encyclopedia Britannica, which was to become the standard in its field. Publication of the Britannica was a major undertaking, with many authorities contributing to it, and with its volumes appearing over a period of three years. Such reference works were often issued in numbers or parts, and later bound into volumes. Often two or more printers would combine their efforts in order to print an encyclopedia, or to issue the complete works of a popular author.

In book illustrations, the wood-cut continued popular in England well into the seventeenth century, although the copper engraving was known there as early as 1588. In the days of Baskerville and Caslon, the copper engraving was well used, and in the nineteenth century it was replaced by the steel engraving. These engravings produced remarkably clear pictures, but the press upon which they were printed advanced little beyond Gutenberg's original invention in the first three centuries of its use. As in library progress, so in the business of manufacturing and distributing books, the nineteenth century was a period of rapid growth and development. In printing methods, in the organization of publishing houses, and in methods of advertising and selling books, the book industry in England reached a high level by 1900. The Victorian world was a literate world, and the market for books, whether the six-penny thriller or the twenty guinea collector's item, was extensive. The English printer and publisher not only met this demand at home, but spread his wares throughout the world, and the twentieth century owes much to these nineteenth century bookmen for both the quantity and the quality of their product.

Bibliography

Bennett, H.S.: English books and readers, 1475-1557.
Cambridge, England, 1952. 336 p.

Bennett, William: John Baskerville. Birmingham, 1937.

Curwen, Henry: A history of book-sellers. London,
1873. 483 p.

Duff, William G.: William Caxton Chicago, 1905. 118 p.

Dury, John: The reformed librarie keeper, (1650).
Chicago, 1906. 71 p.

Edwards, Edward: A statistical view of the principal
public libraries of Europe and America. London,
1849. 48 p.

------Memoirs, of libraries, of museums, and of
archives. London, 1859. 2 vols.

------Free town libraries; their formation, management
and history in Britain, France, Germany and America.
London, 1863. 371 p.

Esdaile, A.J.K.: The British Museum Library. London,
1946. 388 p.

Great Britain. Parliament: Report from a select
committee on public libraries. London, 1849. 317 p.

Greenwood, Thomas: Public libraries; a history of
the movement in England. London, 1890. 586 p.

Hamilton, F.W.: A history of printing in England.
Chicago, 1918. 80 p.

Library association: A century of public libraries,
1850-1950. London, 1950. 27 p.

Minto, John: A history of the public library movement
in Great Britain and Ireland. London, 1932. 366 p.

Munford, W.A.: Penny rate; aspects of British public
library history, 1850-1950. London, 1951. 150 p.

Ogle, John J.: The free library, its history and
present condition. London, 1897. 344 p.

Partridge, R.C.B.: The history of the legal deposit of
books throughout the British Empire. London, 1938.
364 p.

Plomer, Henry R.: A short history of English printing,
1476-1898. London, 1900. 345 p.

Predeek, Albert: A history of libraries in Great
Britain and North America. Chicago, 1947. 177 p.

Rawlings, G.B.: The British Museum Library. London,
1916. 231 p.

Savage, Ernest A.: Old English libraries. London, 1911.
298 p.

Streeter, B.H.: Chained libraries, a survey of four
centuries in the evolution of the English library.
London, 1931. 368 p.

"The foundation of libraries," Cambridge History of
English Literature, IV, 474-497.
Garnett, Richard: "Librarianship in the 17th century,"
in his Essays in Librarianship and Bibliography,
(London, 1899.), p. 174-190.
Houlette, W.D.: "Thomas Bray." Library Quarterly,
IV, (1934), 588-609.
Lyle, Guy R.: "A royal book-collector, George III".
Library Quarterly, III, (1933), 180-191.
McCue, George S.: "Libraries of the London coffee-
houses". Library Quarterly, IV, (1934), 624-627.
Wellard, James H.: "The state of reading among the
working classes of England during the first half of
the nineteenth century." Library Quarterly, V, (1935),
87-100.

VII Printing in Colonial America

The development of printing came only a half century before the discovery of America, and it is not surprising that printing followed closely as European civilization spread to the New World. The Spanish were the first to secure permanent colonies, and their motives in settling them were both religious and economic. They intended to Christianize the natives, and since the printed word was an effective means of spreading and preserving Christianity, a printing press was a logical supplement to the early missionary's equipment. Thus the first printing press in the Americas was established at Mexico City, by Juan Pablos, in or about 1539. Pablos was an agent of Juan Cronberger, a leading printer of Seville in Spain, and from his press there appeared a number of works, including religious volumes published for the Church, primers for the instruction of children, and decrees published for the government. There is some dispute concerning the first printing in Mexico City, and some authorities believe that one Esteban Martin was printing there by 1536, but that is not firmly established. By 1550, Mexico had a typefounder. Antonio Ricardo, an Italian who had learned the art in Mexico City introduced printing into Lima, Peru, in the sixteenth century, but no other Latin American country had printing until late in the seventeenth century.

The first printing in the English colonies in America was done in Massachusetts. The Rev. Jose Glover, who thought that a printing press in the new colony would further the causes of both the church and of Harvard college, arranged for the shipment of a press, and an experienced printer to Cambridge. This press was set up and in operation by early 1639, with the young Matthew Day as the printer. Matthew's father, Stephen Day, is sometimes given as the first American printer, but it is now thought that the elder Day was the me-

chanic who set up the press, while his son was the
actual printer.

The first piece of printing known to have come from
the Day press was a broadside, the Freeman's Oath,
and the first pamphlet was an Almanac for 1639, but
no copies of either have survived. The oldest known
book printed in what is now the United States appeared
from the Day press in 1640, and this was the celebrated Bay Psalm Book, or the Whole Booke of
Psalmes Faithfully Translated into English Metre...
The Day family operated the press until 1649, when,
upon the death of Matthew Day it came under the operation of Samuel Green, who continued it until 1692. Up
to that date more than two hundred books and pamphlets
were published by this one press. They included almanacs, items connected with Harvard College, and books
and pamphlets of a religious nature. In 1675 the first
printing press was established in Boston, and by 1725
most of the larger New England towns had printing
presses.

The second of the English colonies to acquire a
printing press was Pennsylvania, where in 1685 young
William Bradford appeared as a printer sponsored by
the colony's founder, William Penn. Bradford's first
Pennsylvania imprint was also an almanac: America's
Messenger, Being an Almanack for the Year of Grace,
1686. Bradford did not remain long in Penn's good
graces, however, and in a few years he moved to New
York, where in 1693 he established the first press in
that colony. His first known publication was a slap at
the Pennsylvania leaders who had opposed him, and was
entitled: New-England's Spirit of Persecution Trans-
mitted to Pennsilvania... Bradford remained in New
York until his death in 1743, printing more than 400
books and pamphlets during his life-time. He is noted
as one of the colonial era's outstanding printers,
having produced the first New York paper currency, the
first American Book of Common Prayer, the first history of New York, and the first copperplate map of
New York. Bradford also had a share in the establishment of the first paper mill in America, and established
the first printing press in the colony of New Jersey in
1723.

The colony of Virginia had a printing press in 1682, for a brief time, and it is possible that one or two items may have been printed then, but if so there is no record. Instead, the printer, William Nuthead, was ordered by the English government to pack up his press and return to London, which he did. However, he later turned up in Maryland, where by 1689 or possibly earlier, he operated a press at St. Mary's City, making this colony the third to have an active printing establishment. Virginia did not have a permanent printing press until 1730, when William Parks set up operations at Williamsburg. South Carolina followed, with a press at work in Charleston, in 1731, and from that date until the Revolution, this port city was one of the most active printing centers in the colonies. North Carolina had its first press in 1749, with James Davis as the printer, and James Adams became Delaware's first printer in 1761. Georgia had no printer until James Johnston arrived in 1763.

Probably the most outstanding of the colonial printers was a man who is most remembered for his other occupations. Benjamin Franklin was a statesman, philosopher, inventor, and scientist, as well as a journalist and printer, but printing was his first love, and throughout his life he insisted that his vocation was printer. Franklin was born in Boston and at an early age he was apprenticed to an older brother to learn the art of printing. He worked in London for nearly two years as a printer before he returned to Philadelphia. This work was good experience, for the materials and workmanship in the London establishments were superior to those with which he had been acquainted in America.

Shortly after his return, Franklin began his own printing establishment, first as a partner with Hugh Meredith, and later as B. Franklin, Printer. In the next forty years or so of the operation of this press, more than 700 titles were issued from it, exclusive of paper money, broadsides, and newspapers. In 1729, while still in partnership with Meredith, Franklin began publishing The Pennsylvania Gazette, the second weekly newspaper to be established in Philadelphia. Franklin's newspaper proved fairly successful, and led him to begin his second major publication, Poor Richard's Almanac. The almanac was the colonial printer's main stock in trade, and Franklin improved his by writing most of it himself. His witty sayings and sensible advice made Poor Richard a household word for many generations.

The product of the American colonial printer was varied. After 1700, the average printer published a newspaper, sometimes doubling as editor, writer, reporter, pressman and circulation manager, but usually coming in time to the point where he became the editor only and hired journeyman printers to do the actual presswork. Along with the newspaper, the printer usually published an annual almanac which became second only to the Bible in the average colonial home. The almanac contained the calendar for the year, often with elementary astronomical information and the astrological signs. Along with this, it contained witty sayings, home remedies, and general advice on home and farm problems. In addition, each almanac usually gave the names of the officials of the province, and sometimes reprinted the local tax laws. Depending upon the wit and ability of the editor the almanac flourished or failed, some lasting only an issue or two, while others survived a half-century or more. In the later colonial period, the almanac was joined by the provincial register, similar in some respects to the almanac, but containing more political and statistical information about the individual provinces.

Official government publications were important elements in most of the colonial printers' output. In fact, in several instances the early printers were induced to come to the colonies in order to perform the public printing, and in at least one case, in South Carolina, a bonus was offered by the legislature to the first printer who would settle in the colony. The publications of the provincial governments included laws, particularly tax laws, law codes, legislative journals, and the various legal forms needed for the transaction of official business. On the other hand, early colonial printers were quite often controlled by the provincial governments and their Royal governors, and the items printed were sometimes severely censored. Official favoritism too sometimes played a part, and where there were two or more printers in one colony, one might be favored for political reasons, or might win political approval by his good work, as Benjamin Franklin once did early in his printing career. Official printers in each colony were not only favored with the government printing, but were allowed more license in what they did print. A celebrated case in colonial legal history was that of Peter Zenger, who published some attacks against the local government in New York. For this he was imprisoned under a charge of libel. At his trial he won acquittal. This case established a legal precedent in similar cases of libel, providing that the jury should be the judges of both the law and the facts in a particular case. The Zenger case is considered a forward step in the development of freedom of the press.

The colonial printer, when not engaged with newspapers and governmental publications, turned out a variety of broadsides, pamphlets and books. The broadsides were numerous, usually little more than circulars announcing meetings, or giving the results of court cases, or proposing some change in governmental procedures. They were printed on one side of a sheet only, and were designed to be posted. In effect they were supplements to the newspapers, and sometimes they were actually called extras. The pamphlets were usually political or religious, and the numbers published by all the colonial presses undoubtedly ran into the thousands. The pamphlets were usually hastily printed, poorly sewn, undoubtedly widely read, and often quickly forgotten. Certainly there were many more of them printed than have survived, and one writer estimates that for every one preserved there must have been four or five that were lost. In books, religion led the list of publications of the colonial printer, amounting to almost two-fifths of all colonial printing. Collected sermons were especially popular in New England, but were widely printed and reprinted in all the colonies. Law codes, legal form books, legislative journals, and official manuals accounted for another fifth of the printing, as did literature in all its forms. Most of the literary works published were editions of the classics, with a few contemporary European and English authors, and a very few American items. The relatively small percentage of literary publications was probably due to the fact that such items could be purchased in English editions cheaper than they could be reprinted in America. This was true also of the Bible, of which there were very few editions published by colonial printers. The social sciences together, including history, economics, education and political science, accounted for the final fifth, with the exception of about three percent made up of publications in science and the arts. Among the histories were several volumes on the development of the individual colonies, and many more on early relations with the Indians. Some books went through numerous editions, as, for example, the New England Primer, which was printed in more than thirty editions and millions of copies between 1690 and 1830. The Office and Authority of a Justice of Peace, a legal handbook, went through forty editions between 1710 and 1800. All told, at least 18,300 different publications were issued by colonial American printers, counting a full year of a newspaper as only one item, and some estimates place the actual figure, including items no longer extant, as high as 80,000 separate publications.

The earliest newspaper printed in the English colonies was an issue of Public Occurences, published on September 25, 1690, by Benjamin Harris in Boston. The provincial government objected to the contents of this first issue, and banned further publications. Some fourteen years passed before another printer became bold enough to issue a newspaper, and this time it was begun with authority of the government, and survived as the Boston News-Letter. The publisher was John Campbell, and the first issue was dated April 24, 1704. The name was apt, for it was little more than a letter about chief news events in the colonies and elsewhere. It came out weekly, or sometimes every two weeks, and it managed not only to meet the approval of the provincial authorities, but actually secured a subsidy on one or two occasions. It never became financially successful, and as late as 1719, the publisher complained that he had less than 300 paying subscribers. Other early newspapers were the Boston Gazette, (1719); the New England Courant (1721) also of Boston; the American Weekly Mercury (1722), and Franklin's Pennsylvania Gazette (1729), both of Philadelphia. New York's first paper was the Weekly Journal, founded in 1733, but this was preceded by a few months by both the Virginia Gazette, of Williamsburg, and the South Carolina Gazette, of Charleston. In all, more than a hundred different newspapers, most of them short-lived, were published in the thirteen colonies before the Revolution.

The colonial newspaper soon developed into a political weapon, and all sides in the provincial political squabbles took advantage of the press in presenting their viewpoints. As the Revolution approached, some took up a staunch position in defense of the King, while others just as strongly defended the colonists. The contents of the average colonial newspaper ran strongly to political tracts, with literary works in serial form being also fairly common. News as such was usually weeks or months old, and made up only a small portion of the newspaper space. Official decrees sometimes made up most of a single issue, particularly when the provincial legislature was in session. Later in the eighteenth century advertising developed, and contributed to the financial stability of the newspaper. Most of the advertisements were of the classified type, short and to the point, calling attention to goods for sale, a runaway slave, or a delinquent wife who had left the advertiser's bed and board. In the late colonial period, the larger merchants would sometimes take a half or full column to list their choice wares, item by item, and all "just arrived from England on the latest packet." Editorial policies were strong, and rival printers often used vicious language in attacking each other, usually over fictitious names. Readers contributed their ideas and opinions in long letters to the editors, often signed by pseudonyms, such as "Publius," or "Pro Bono Publico." Lists of ships arriving and departing, and occasionally stage coach and mail schedules were printed, either in advertisements, or as a public service. Most newspapers were only four pages, and ranged in size from about ten by fourteen inches, to about half the size of a modern newspaper.

The first American magazine, published for about three months in 1741 by Andrew Bradford of Philadelphia, was appropriately enough entitled American Magazine. However, like most periodicals of its day it had a long sub-title: A Monthly View of the Political State of the British Colonies. Benjamin Franklin followed with his General Magazine and Historical Chronicle only a few days after Bradford's magazine, and this periodical lasted six months. Both were really supplements to their publishers' newspapers, and as such carried little appeal beyond their news value. Between 1741 and 1775 no less than seventeen different magazines were started in the colonies, but most lasted only a short time, and none survived the Revolution. The American colonial magazines lacked one prime ingredient--writers. They could not compete with the several good British periodicals in content, and since timeliness was of little importance, the American magazine could not attract an audience.

Throughout the colonial period the printing press in use was little changed from that developed by Gutenberg two centuries earlier. Most presses, or their component parts, were bought in England, although Christopher Sauer, a noted printer of Germantown, Pennsylvania, built his own press, and possibly a very few others did in the later colonial period. The type used came also from England or Germany until about 1770 when the Sauers and also Abel Buell of Connecticut began to cast their own type. Paper, on the other hand, was made in the colonies as early as 1690, when William Rittenhouse, a German papermaker, began a paper mill for William Bradford near Philadelphia. The paper industry grew slowly, but by the Revolution much of the paper used in the colonies was made here, especially in Pennsylvania. Benjamin Franklin was very much interested in the manufacture of paper, and is supposed to have aided in the establishment of no less than eighteen paper making factories from Virginia to New York. This early American paper, like that of Europe down to the nineteenth century, was made of cotton and linen rags. The ink used was made of linseed oil and lampblack, and although both these ingredients were available in the later colonial period, it seems that most printers preferred to buy ready-mixed inks from England. Franklin and Bradford, among a few other printers, did at times make their own printing ink, but they too purchased much from England, as surviving records show. In the early days, the printer's working staff consisted largely of his wife and family, but as his business grew he took on apprentices and sometimes hired extra journeymen. The largest printing establishments before the Revolution had four presses and a force of ten or twelve typesetters and pressmen. Wages paid to skilled printers were comparatively high, and they were considered to be among the most important of the skilled workers.

The position of the printer in colonial society was an interesting one. He was quite often an influential member of the colony in which he lived, and sometimes he grew into relative economic wealth as well. Franklin was, of course, no average printer, but William Bradford, Lewis Timothy of South Carolina, Samuel Green of Massachusetts, and a dozen or more other printers were important citizens in their home towns and provinces. Part of this was due to their newspapers, which, despite occasional control and censorship, exercised considerable influence in colonial politics. But the printer himself was often a self-educated man who took a natural position of community leadership, over and above the importance of his newspaper. A book-store was often attached to the printing shop, and since the printer was about the only stationer available, he had many irons in the fire. An interesting sidelight on colonial printing is the number of women who took an active part in the printing business. Franklin freely acknowledged the help of his wife in the print-shop during the early days of their marriage, and in Charleston, Anne Timothy took over and operated the press several years after the death of her husband, Lewis Timothy, and before her son, Peter Timothy, was old enough to handle the business. Dinah Nuthead, the widow of William Nuthead, operated a printing house in Annapolis, Maryland, for a few years after 1695, and Ann Franklin, sister-in-law of Benjamin, operated a press in Newport, Rhode Island, after 1758. Several families included printers in several generations, and the descendants of Samuel Green of Massachusetts were printers and publishers for nearly two centuries.

As the American Revolution got under way, the colonial printer soon became an important part of it. The Stamp Act of 1765 involved directly the publications and printed forms produced by the printer, and, as the differences became more pronounced, it was the printer who

kept the people informed of developments through his
newspapers and broadsides. The actions of the Conti-
nental Congress, and the retaliatory actions of the
British Parliament were hot news events that were published from Maine to Georgia. The Committees of
Correspondence made full use of the printing press in
distributing their news from colony to colony. Particularly important was the pamphlet. One pamphlet in
particular, Thomas Paine's Common Sense, coming as
it did in January, 1776, and selling many thousand
copies, changed an economic dispute into a war for
independence, simply by pointing out to the Americans
that independence was possible, and that the dawn of an
American empire was at hand. It is indeed hard to im-
agine a successful American Revolution without the aid
of the provincial printing presses. And the colonial
printer, taking sides as he did, either with King or
country--for several of them did remain loyal to
Britain--was worth a regiment or two at least to the
cause he favored. Printers on both sides suffered
during the war through destruction or seizure of their
presses and shortages of paper, ink and help. But in
the end, the importance of the printer and his product
was fully appreciated, and when in 1787 the new United
States Constitution was written, prominent among its
articles was one guaranteeing freedom of the press.

Bibliography

Kimber, Sydney A.: The story of an old press. Cam-
    bridge, Mass., 1937. 43 p.
Lehman-Haupt, Hellmut: The book in America. New
    York, 1939. 453 p.
McMurtrie, Douglas C.: The beginnings of the American
    newspaper. Chicago, 1935. 36 p.
------ The book; the story of printing and bookmaking.
    New York, 1943. 676 p.
------ A history of printing in the United States: Middle
    and South Atlantic States. New York, 1936. 462 p.
Mott, Frank L.: A history of American magazines,
    1741-1850. New York, 1930. 848 p.
Orcutt, W.D.: The magic of the book. Boston, 1930.
    315 p. (See pp. 17-62 on early New England printing.)

Oswald, John C.: Benjamin Franklin, printer. Garden City, 1917. 244 p.

------ Printing in the Americas. New York, 1937. 565 p.

Richardson, L.N.: A history of early American magazines, 1741-1789. New York, 1931. 414 p.

Roden, Robert F.: The Cambridge press, 1638-1692. New York, 1905. 193 p.

Stillwell, Margaret B.: Incunabula and Americana. New York, 1931.

Thomas, Isaiah: History of printing in America. Albany, N.Y., 1874. 2 vols.

Weeks, Lyman H.: A history of paper manufacturing in the United States, 1690-1916. New York, 1916. 352 p.

Winterich, John T.: Early American books and printing. Boston, 1935. 256 p.

Wroth, Lawrence C.: The colonial printer. Portland, Maine, 1938. 368 p.

Table II
Notable Early American Printers†

Date	Printer	Location
1639	Matthew Day	Cambridge, Massachusetts
1649	Samuel Green	Cambridge, Massachusetts
1675	John Foster	Boston, Massachusetts
1685	William Bradford	Philadelphia, Pennsylvania
1689	William Nuthead	St. Mary's City, Maryland
1693	William Bradford	New York, New York
1709	Thomas Short	New London, Connecticut
1723	William Bradford	Perth Amboy, New Jersey
1727	James Franklin	Newport, Rhode Island
1728	Benjamin Franklin	Philadelphia, Pennsylvania
1730	William Parks	Williamsburg, Virginia
1731	George Webb	Charleston, South Carolina
1733	Lewis Timothy	Charleston, South Carolina
1738	Christopher Sauer	Germantown, Pennsylvania
1749	James Davis	Newbern, North Carolina
1751	James Parker	Woodbridge, New Jersey
1756	Daniel Fowle	Portsmouth, New Hampshire
1761	James Adams	Wilmington, Delaware
1763	James Johnston	Savannah, Georgia
1764	Denis Braud	New Orleans, Louisiana
1783	William C. Wells	St. Augustine, Florida
1787	John Bradford	Lexington, Kentucky
1791	George Roulstone	Rogersville, Tennessee
1793	William Maxwell	Cincinnati, Ohio
1797	John McCall	Detroit, Michigan
1799	Andrew Marschalk	Natchez, Mississippi

†This list includes only the first printers in the various states before 1800, and a few of the other more important colonial printers.

VIII Libraries in Colonial America

The American colonists were largely engaged in making a living, with religious and political interests taking up most of their free time, but a few of them were interested enough in books and education to form libraries--college, private, and semi-public. None of these colonial libraries reached a large size, and it is doubtful whether any of them had any considerable cultural influence, but the fact that they existed is noteworthy, and in them we see the beginnings of American library history. The colonial colleges, particularly Harvard and Yale, had useful book collections, and a few individuals collected rather valuable private libraries, but for the most part the efforts at public library service, though present, were meager and ineffective.

It is interesting to note that a college, and a college library, were planned for the infant colony of Virginia, along with a school for the education of the Indians, but the Indian War of 1622 put an end to these philanthropic and educational designs. Instead, Virginia had to wait another seventy years for the founding of its first college, William and Mary, and even longer for its college library. In Massachusetts, however, Harvard College Library almost preceded the founding of the college itself. In fact, the college name comes from John Harvard, who in 1638 gave the college some 380 books and a small cash endowment. Harvard's library grew very slowly, and its seventeenth century contents were largely theological, since the college of that day was mainly a training school for ministers. In 1764, with the college more than a century and a quarter old, the library still contained less than 5,000 volumes. In that year it was burned, with almost a total loss of its book collection. After this tragedy, friends of the college came to its aid, and the provincial legislature voted L2000 to replace the burned Harvard Hall. In

addition, a popular subscription raised almost another
L 1000, and many gifts of money and books were received, so that rapid growth was experienced, and by
1775 the library was back to its former size. According to its catalog of 1790, the Harvard library was still
largely theological, but it contained a variety of historical, scientific and literary works as well. In literature,
the English authors were fairly well represented, including Shakespeare, Milton, Spenser, Chaucer, Pope and
Dryden, and European works were represented by Boccaccio, Voltaire, La Fontaine and Rabelais. Needless
to say, the classics were present and most of them
were in Greek or Latin rather than in translations.

Yale College also began with a collection of books.
The eleven ministers who, in 1700, organized a society
for the formation of a college in New Haven, each made
a donation of books, and in the next decade other donations increased the collection to several hundred
volumes. In 1714, a group of English gentlemen, including Sir Isaac Newton, made a donation of 800
volumes to Yale, through the good offices of Jeremiah
Dummer, then the agent of Connecticut in London. In
1717, Rev. Elihu Yale, for whom the college was named,
gave 300 books to the college library, and in 1733, the
Rev. Dr. George Berkeley of London sent a gift of a
thousand volumes, including many valuable folios. By
1765, Yale had a library of about 4,000 volumes, including besides theological works, large collections of
history, classics philosophy and mathematics. The
President of the College noted in that year that the collection contained "not many authors who have wrote
within these thirty years."

William and Mary College, in Virginia, was the second
oldest in the colonies, having been founded in 1693, but
its library grew slowly during the eighteenth century.
Aid for the college library was received from time to
time from the Virginia legislature, but this aid was not
very much. Several gifts and bequests of books added
to the William and Mary collection, but of these only
the library of James Blair, a president of the college,
which was donated in 1743, was of any notable size. It
is doubtful whether the William and Mary library
numbered more than 2,000 volumes in 1775.

Among other colonial colleges, the library of King's College (later Columbia University) in New York, was formed in 1757, largely on a gift from the Rev. Dr. Bristowe of London. Oxford University Library sent a gift of duplicates from its collection, and several British noblemen made gifts of books to the college library. Unfortunately, during the Revolution, this collection was destroyed by British soldiers, who used its quarters as a military hospital. In 1764, the library of the College of New Jersey, (later Princeton) contained about 1200 books, all gifts. The library of the College of Rhode Island (later Brown University), contained only 250 volumes in 1772, while that of Dartmouth College was also insignificant before the Revolution. The only other college library dating from before the Revolution was at the University of Pennsylvania. This collection was small, but it did survive the Revolution, and was even enlarged by a gift from the King of France, mostly scientific and mathematical works from the royal printing office.

In all the colonial colleges, the libraries were reference collections, and were more for the use of faculty than for students. In fact, students were expected, at least during their first years in college, to study only their textbooks, and to own those. Younger faculty members were usually in charge of the college libraries, which were kept open only two or three hours daily.

Probably the first attempt at a public library in the colonies came in 1656 when Capt. Robert Keayne of Boston willed his library to the city for public use. In order to house the library, and also provide for a town hall and meeting place, Keayne provided funds for a building, and this was erected and in use by 1658. This first Boston Public Library remained small, and just how much it was used is uncertain. But it was public property, and on several occasions the town fathers of Boston took notice of its presence, as for example in 1702, when they requested John Barnard, Jr., to prepare a catalog of the collection. In 1711, the town hall was burned, but fortunately most of the books were saved. Another fire in 1747, however, completely destroyed it, and only one book, Samuel Mather's A Testimony from the Scripture against Idolatry and Superstition, is known to have survived from this first American public library. Other towns, particularly in New England, may have had similar publicly owned book collections, but they were not public libraries in the modern sense of the word.

Rev. Thomas Bray, the English religious leader who had sponsored parish libraries in England, also encouraged and promoted the establishment of semi-public church libraries in the American colonies. This was done through the Society for the Propagation of the Gospel in Foreign Parts, an English missionary organization. Libraries were established around 1700 in Anglican churches from Charleston, South Carolina, to Newport, Rhode Island. Usually these parish libraries were small collections of books religious in nature, and placed in the care of the parish vestry for the use of both ministers and laymen. There is little evidence of any great use of these books, and the idea did not long survive the death of Rev. Bray, although in some cases the books survived in individual church libraries. Any connection between these libraries and the later public library movement in the United States is difficult to perceive.

The first successful attempt at semi-public library service came through the establishment of the social or subscription libraries. The first of these were established in the second quarter of the eighteenth century, and they followed in general the pattern of similar organizations in England. Benjamin Franklin is usually given credit for beginning the first American one in Philadelphia in 1731. He and a small group of friends began the Philadelphia Library Company, and in the first year of its operation some fifty members, including doctors, lawyers, tradesmen and skilled workers, paid L2 each for membership. Franklin sent to Europe for books, and on his later visits to England and France personally selected and sent back many valuable volumes. At first the library was kept in the home of a member, but in 1740 it was moved into a room of the State House, a public building now known as Independence Hall, and it was opened a few hours weekly for public use, although only members could remove books. In 1773, the Philadelphia Library Company, now joined by several other library associations, moved to Carpenters' Hall. There during the Revolution and the later Constitutional Convention, it served the founding fathers of the United States as virtually the only library available. In 1789 it moved into a building of its own, and it has survived to the present where it forms an important part of the Philadelphia Public Library system.

Other colonial towns soon followed the lead of Philadelphia in establishing subscription libraries. There were four in Connecticut before 1740, and about fifty in New England before 1780. Some of them were merely voluntary associations but generally they took some form of legal contract, either between individuals, or in the form of a corporation chartered by the provincial government. The Redwood Library, in Newport, Rhode Island, was one of the most important of these early social libraries. It was operated by the Redwood Library Company, chartered by the Rhode Island provincial assembly in 1747. In 1750 it moved into its own quarters, probably the first building constructed solely for library purposes in the English colonies. This library was fortunate in having a librarian from 1755 to 1775 in the person of Dr. Ezra Stiles, a minister in Newport who devoted a few hours of his time each week to keeping the library in return for the privilege of using the books. In 1748, the Charleston, S.C., Library Society was formed, and it has been in continuous existence since that date, although many of its books have been destroyed by fires at different times during its history. New York Society Library opened in 1754, and Providence, Rhode Island began a similar institution in 1758. By the Revolution most of the larger towns in the colonies and many of the smaller ones had social or subscription libraries.

The social library was a private library strictly speaking, but it was generally open to any interested reader who could afford the relatively small membership fee. It was sometimes open, as was the Philadelphia Library Company, to any reader who cared to come during the hours that it was open. It often contained local and other provincial newspapers, as well as periodicals from England and possibly other European countries. Its bookstock consisted of the books that its members wanted to read; sometimes they were heavily weighted in the direction of theological works and the classics, and in other cases they contained more contemporary literature or political and economic works, depending upon the tastes of their readers. Ordinarily the collection was in charge of some member who devoted a small amount of time to it, or perhaps to an interested non-member who received the use of the collection for keeping it open a few hours each week. Only rarely was there a paid librarian, but usually several of the members were interested in building up the library, and often the bookstock came to contain many valuable items through their collecting activities. All things considered, the social library was the nearest thing to public library service that was available in the colonial period.

Private libraries were almost as scarce in the colonial period as their public counterparts, but there were a few notable examples of book collecting among the early leaders in the colonies. In New England some of the best private libraries were gathered by ministers, whereas in the southern colonies it was the wealthy planters who had time and means to become bibliophiles. In all of the colonies, especially in the later colonial period, the merchant sometimes became a book collector and amassed a sizable private library, and in a few cases governmental officials in the colonies did likewise. In Massachusetts, the seventeenth century minister, Increase Mather, collected a library of nearly 3,000 volumes, while his son, Cotton Mather, who inherited only a part of his father's library, built his own to more than 4,000 volumes. Most of the books in both of these libraries were theological, but there were small numbers of classical authors and works of history in each. Incidentally, Cotton Mather wrote and published more than 400 books and pamphlets on religious and historical subjects, making him one of the most prolific writers America has ever produced. John Sharp, of New York, built up a large library for his day, mainly of religious works, and gave it in 1713 to the city for public use, but there is no record of its ever having been so used. In the same year, Rev. Alexander Innes left a sizeable collection of books to the Episcopal churches of New York and New Jersey, and Samuel Johnson, early president of King's College, collected a large private library, particularly strong in English literature, the classics and history. Probably the most important single private library of the colonial period was that collected by James Logan of Philadelphia. This gentleman, who had served as Chief Justice and as Lieutenant Governor of Pennsylvania, collected more than 3,000 volumes before his death in 1751. The Loganian collection was strong in scientific works, mathematics, astronomy, and "natural philosophy" as physics was then called. It eventually became a part of the Philadelphia Library Company and added considerably to the importance of that institution. The Redwood Library of Newport was built around a nucleus collection brought together by Abraham Redwood, a merchant and lawyer of that city. Thomas Prince, a minister of Boston, formed an important collection of books and manuscripts relating for the most part to New England history, and deposited them in the Old South Church in Boston before his death in 1758. These works later became the property of the Boston Public Library.

In the South, the most important private library of the colonial period was that of William Byrd of Westover, in Virginia, who lived from about 1670 to 1740. His father had built up a large estate, and had started to collect books, but it was the son who enlarged the collection to nearly 4,000 volumes. The William Byrd library is interesting because of the nature of its contents and its contrast with the New England ministers' libraries. Byrd was a planter, lawyer and public official, as well as a writer, and his library reflected the cultural level and interests of the Virginia planter. Of the 4,000 volumes, 523 were in Latin and 230 in French. Almost a fourth of the collection was made up of works of history, another fourth of classical literature, and about ten per cent each in English literature, law and science. Conspicuous by their absence were theological works, except for the Latin works of some early Church writers, and several works associated with the Church of England. The Byrd library was probably the best collection of literature in the colonies.

In both North and South Carolina there were several private libraries of note, though none quite equalled that of William Byrd. Gabriel Johnston, governor of North Carolina from 1734 to 1752, had a distinguished library, particularly strong in biography, travel and history, but including books on medicine, economics, literature and law as well. This library passed to Gabriel Johnston's nephew, Samuel Johnston, also a later governor of the state, and under his attention the family library grew considerably. It remained in the family throughout the eighteenth and nineteenth centuries, and at the end of the Civil War it was estimated to contain about 4500 volumes. Edward Moseley, Col. James Innes, John Hodgson, and James Iredell were other colonial North Carolinians with relatively large private libraries. In South Carolina, Henry Laurens, merchant and planter of Charleston, developed a large family library, augmented by books which he personally selected on his trips to Europe. Other South Carolina planters and ministers, including especially the Izards, Middletons and Rutledges, had notable libraries, which remained in the same family for several generations.

Most of the colonial leaders, whether in business, church or government, had smaller collections of books in their homes, and the men who lead the colonies into the Revolution were well-read. Their speeches and writings abound with allusions to authors both classical and contemporary, and most of these works were undoubtedly in their own private libraries. Among those leaders known to have had sizeable private book collections were John Hancock and John Adams of Massachusetts, the Livingstones of New York, the Pinkneys and Carrolls of Maryland, Jefferson and Madison in Virginia, John Rutledge and the Pinckneys of South Carolina, and many others. The library of George Washington at Mount Vernon was not large in comparison to some of the others, but it was well-rounded. After his marriage to Martha Custis, Washington ordered from London a collection of children's books for his stepchildren.

One other type of library service developed in the late colonial period. This was the rental or circulating library associated with printshops and bookstores. Particularly after about 1765 it became possible, in the larger colonial towns, to rent books from the booksellers

for a small fee. Rentals were for individual books, or
for the use of books over a given period of time, and
rates for the most part were low. Possibly the first
of these circulating libraries was opened by William
Rind, of Annapolis, Maryland, in 1762. He proposed to
allow his customers the use of two books at a time for
an annual fee of 27 shillings. His venture was unsuccessful and was discontinued in 1764. Boston, Philadelphia, New York and Charleston had similar ventures
in or shortly after 1765, with varying degrees of success. One in Boston, operated by John Mein, was particularly ambitious and published a catalog of some
1200 volumes available for rent at the rate of twenty-
eight shillings per year for all that one could read one
volume at a time. Mein was a Loyalist, however, and
he ran into political difficulties that soon put him out of
business. The circulating library did not achieve success before the Revolution, but it did add a small a-
mount to the facilities available to the colonial reader.

Closely related to both printing and libraries in the
colonial world was the bookstore. At first the printer
was also a bookseller, and throughout the period many
of the most important bookstores were connected with
printshops or binderies, but in later years the book-
store emerged as a separate business. The stock of
the bookstore varied somewhat from that of the colonial libraries. There was a strong emphasis on almanacs,
Bibles, and religious works, since these were the most
readily sold, but there was a wide variety of other
items available for the discriminating purchaser. A
checklist of books advertised for sale in the South Carolina Gazette, for example, includes Psalm books,
primers, horn-books, spelling books, prayer books, and
dictionaries. Books were available in Greek, Latin,
French, German and Spanish as well as English. Sermons
were apparently in great demand, as were also the various commentaries on the Bible, but works were also
advertised on history, mathematics, astronomy, geography, and architecture. Practical works and fiction were
also available in the bookstores. The booksellers also
sold magazines and took subscriptions for both English
and American periodicals. Book auctions were common,
both as a means of disposing of accumulated bookstocks,
and for the sale of private libraries.

In general, the average colonial American was not a literary man, but the men who emerged as his leaders generally were. The ministers, public officials, lawyers and college teachers were well educated. Moreover, the leading planters and merchants were often ardent readers and pursued literary tastes with both their minds and their pocket books. From their own private libraries, and from the book stores in the coastal towns, they had access to most books available in England at that time. That they made effective use of them is evidenced in the Declaration of Independence, the Constitution, and the numerous journals, diaries and books that have come down to us from the colonial period.

Bibliography

Bolton, C.K.: American library history. Chicago, 1911. 13 p.
------ Proprietary and subscription libraries. Chicago, 1912. 10 p.
Cohen, Hennig, ed.: The South Carolina Gazette, 1732-1775. Columbia, 1953. 273 p.
Conner, Martha: Outline of the history of the development of the American public library. Chicago, 1931. 179 p.
Gray, Austin K.: Benjamin Franklin's library. New York 1936. 80 p.
Keep, Austin B.: History of the New York Society Library, with an introductory chapter on libraries in colonial New York. New York, 1908. 607 p.
Lehmann-Haupt, Hellmut: The book in America. New York, 1939. 453 p. (This edition has a chapter on library history).
Morison, Samuel E.: The Puritan Pronaos: studies in the intellectual life of New England in the seventeenth century. New York, 1936. (See especially pp. 110-147).
Potter, A.C.: Descriptive and historical notes on the library of Harvard University, Cambridge, 1903. 43 p.
Predeek, Albert: A history of libraries in Great Britain and North America. Chicago, 1947. 177 p.
Shera, Jesse H.: Foundations of the public library. Chicago, 1949. 308 p.
Shores, Louis: Origins of the American college library, 1638-1800. New York, 1935. 290 p.

Thompson, C.S.: Evolution of the Amercian public library, 1653-1876. Washington, 1952. 297 p.
U.S. Bureau of Education: Public libraries in the United States of America, their history, condition and management. Washington, 1876. 1187 p.
Wright, Thomas Goddard: Literary culture in early New England, 1620-1730. New Haven, 1920. 322 p.

Borden, A.K.: Seventeenth century American Libraries. Library Quarterly, II, (1932), 137-147.
Canavan, Michael J.: The Old Boston Public Library, 1656-1747, Proceedings of the Colonial Society of Massachusetts, XII, (March, 1908), 116-133.
Houlette, William D.: Parish libraries and the work of Rev. Thomas Bray, Library Quarterly, IV, (Oct. 1934), 588-609.
Keys, Thomas E.: The colonial library and the development of sectional differences. Library Quarterly, VIII, (1938), 373-390.
Spain, Frances L.: Libraries of South Carolina, their origins and early history. Library Quarterly, XVII, (1947), 28-42.
Steiner, B.C.: Rev. Thomas Bray and his American libraries, American Historical Review, II, (1896), 59-75.
Tuttle, J.H.: The libraries of the Mathers, American Antiquarian Society, Proceedings, XX, (1910), 269-356.
Weeks, Stephen B.: Libraries and literature of North Carolina in the eighteenth century, American Historical Association, Annual Report, 1895, 171-269.

IX American Libraries, 1775-1850

The Revolution had a disastrous effect on many of the early American libraries. From Boston to Charleston libraries were scattered, destroyed or stolen, and only a few managed to escape unharmed. Aside from loss by military action, the libraries also lacked attention, and for a generation there was no concerted effort to rebuild or improve them. Following the Peace of Paris in 1783 there was some progress, but it was not until after 1790 that books, newspapers, magazines and libraries returned to their prewar levels, and began to forge ahead.

Though forced to move from Cambridge to Concord during the early part of the war, Harvard College saved its books, and even added to them with funds allocated by the state legislature, and from books confiscated from Tories. By 1800, Harvard's library was approaching 13,000 volumes. Yale's library suffered considerably during the Revolution, and in 1791 its catalog contained but 2700 volumes. Princeton's Nassau Hall, which housed the college library, was occupied by both British and American troops at different times, and served successively as barracks, prison, hospital and stable. After the War, the state of New Jersey voted a sum of money to aid in restoring the war-damaged buildings, and the college began levying an annual library fee for the purchase of books. At the turn of the century, Princeton had 3000 books, only to lose them in a fire in 1802. Columbia University (King's College) had most of its books stolen during the British occupation of New York, but a few of them were returned by the order of the British commander. In the 1790's, the New York legislature also helped Columbia and by 1800 its library was once again in a respectable condition. In Rhode Island, Brown University (College of Rhode Island) had its library moved to the country for safekeeping during the War, and when it was returned, only about 500 volumes were found to be usable. In 1784, John Brown made a donation of 1400 volumes to the college library, a gift considered so important at the time that the name of the college was changed in his honor. These examples are typical of the effects of the Revolutionary war on the college libraries, and of their conditions in the decades immediately following. In the ensuing half-century, however, colleges were to increase rapidly in number, and their libraries in size, so that by 1850, the average college library was a great improvement over its colonial ancestor.

The early nineteenth century saw the founding of a number of the important colleges. Bowdoin College in Maine began with a small collection of books in 1802, but in 1811 it received a gift of 4000 volumes from James Bowdoin, its prime benefactor. Amherst College in Massachusetts, began in 1821 with a single case of books, but by 1832, after a drive for donations, its library reached 3000 volumes, and was suitably housed in a room in the chapel building. By 1855 it could boast 12,000 books and a building of its own. Hamilton College, in Clinton, New York, was founded in 1812, and inherited a small library from an earlier academy. A campaign for donations of books and funds was not too successful, and the library numbered only 1600 volumes in 1826. Another small college library, that of Dickinson College in Pennsylvania, began in 1783, but with insufficient funds and no large donations, it grew so slowly that in 1850 it still numbered only about 5,000 volumes.

Among the newer state universities established after the Revolution were those of Virginia, North Carolina and South Carolina. North Carolina's University library began in 1795 with a small collection including fourteen volumes donated by the Governor of the state, William R. Davie. Other donations followed, all of them small, and in the 1820's the president of the University, Dr. Joseph Caldwell, sent to England to purchase almost a thousand volumes for the college library, along with some scientific equipment. It was not until 1850 that the library moved into a separate building, and at that time the collection numbered a few less than 7000 volumes. South Carolina's University library opened in 1805, with an appropriation of 3,000 dollars from the state legislature for books. It continued to receive support from the state, moved into its own building in 1841, and by mid-century it contained more than 12,000 books, forming the largest and most important library south of Virginia. Not only was it impressive in numbers, but many of its works were rare. The University of Virginia, opening in 1825, had the benefit of the advice of ex-President Thomas Jefferson in selecting and organizing its library. Although Jefferson's own library had been purchased by the Library of Congress, President James Madison donated his library of 2500 volumes to the University of Virginia and added a bequest of 1500 dollars. Many other gifts came from Virginia's planter families, and by 1850, its university library contained more than 30,000 volumes, making it one of the best in the nation.

Although Harvard, Yale and possibly one or two other college libraries reached a point where assistant librarians were employed, most of them had only one person. As in the colonial days, these individuals were usually either junior members of the faculty, or retired faculty. Organization of the collection was for the most part limited to location symbols, such as "Alcove 5, Shelf B, Book 2", although there was usually a subject or language division by alcoves. Hours of opening were sometimes limited to a single hour a day, and circulation rules were quite strict. In some cases, only upper classmen were permitted to remove books from the college library, and then only upon recommendation of a faculty member. Usually the library was housed in a room or wing of a college building, although by 1850 the larger colleges were moving their book collections into separate buildings. Generally speaking, the college library was still a reference library, with its basic purpose that of preserving books rather than using them.

In addition to the regular college library, there was often another type of library on the average college campus. This was the literary society collection. It became the custom in the nineteenth century for each campus to have one or more societies, usually two, with their own meeting halls, and their own libraries. In time, many of these literary society libraries grew to be larger than the college libraries and with valuable gifts from their alumni, they became important, scholarly collections. They had student librarians, and were strictly for student use, meeting their library needs much more effectively than the main college library. In the later nineteenth century, however, most of these society libraries were merged with the college libraries.

Somewhat akin to the college library, and even more important from the reference point of view, were the scientific society libraries that developed in the larger cities during the early nineteenth century. The oldest of these was the American Philosophical Society, which was founded in Philadelphia in 1743, and which by 1850 contained over 15,000 books and nearly as many pamphlets. Franklin Institute, also in Philadelphia, was founded in 1824 as a scientific society particularly interested in the physical sciences, and its library was nearly as large as that of the Philosophical Society. In Boston, the American Academy of Arts and Sciences (1780), and the Boston Society of Natural History (1831), each had libraries of more than 10,000 volumes, while the Massachusetts Horticultural Society (1829) had a library only one-fourth as large at the mid-century. The New York Academy of Sciences (1818) and the Albany Institute of Science (1824) each had respectable libraries of their own, and throughout the New England, Middle Atlantic, and Middle Western states, the major towns by 1850 usually supported one or more scientific societies. Strictly speaking, these scientific libraries were only for the use of members, but in general practice any serious user could obtain access to them.

The period after the Revolution to 1850 saw rapid development of the social or subscription library. These libraries had begun to achieve popularity even before the Revolution, but after about 1785, they increased rapidly in numbers, size and importance. In fact, between the Revolution and 1850 more than a thousand social libraries were established in the six New England states alone. Most small towns had at least one, and the larger urban areas supported two or more. Social libraries were usually general in character, but there were a number of mechanics' libraries, lyceum libraries, young men's libraries, and even factory workers' libraries. A few of them were organized along special subject lines, such as theological, historical, agricultural, medical or military collections. About twenty were for children only. As in the colonial period, the social library operated on a subscription basis, and numbers of members varied from a dozen or so up to several hundred. In book stock, the libraries ranged from less than a hundred volumes up to 10,000 or more, and in a few cases, up to 50,000. The books were generally popular, but they reflected the reading tastes of their clientele, so that some of them ran rather heavily to theological works and the classics, while others concentrated on history, biography, travel and literature. Some completely excluded fiction, while others included up to a fourth of their book stock in this newly popular variety of reading. Science, economics, agriculture, sociology and law made up only a small percentage of titles, but some of the social libraries made up for this lack by supplying the latest of English and American periodicals.

The organization of social libraries was usually very simple. There was ordinarily little or no attempt at arrangement or classification. Housing was arranged in a public building, a member's home or business, or in a few cases in separate buildings. Hours of opening were few, and a voluntary or paid attendent charged books and checked on their return. Selection of new books was in the hands of a committee of members, although it often fell to one person, either by election or self-appointment. As early as 1793 a pamphlet had been written to advise the book selectors for social libraries on the best methods of obtaining books, and the best books to be selected. This was the Selected Catalogue of Some of the Most Esteemed Publications in the English Language Proper to Form a Social Library, by Thaddeus Mason Harris, a young man who had served for a short time as librarian at Harvard. His pamphlet was one of the earliest works on book selection, and as such it is most interesting. He divided all books into three classes; memory, reason, and imagination. The first class included all phases of history, biography and travel; the second, science, philosophy, and religion; and the third, poetry, drama, fiction and art. In all he recommended only 81 titles. The social libraries bought only a few titles a year on an average, but collectively they made up an important book market, so that by 1800 book publishers and dealers were offering them special discounts in order to secure their trade.

One popular type of subscription library was that designed for the use of workers or apprentices. These were intended primarily for the younger workers in the factories and trades, and though there were a few factory libraries for the girl employees of the New England cotton mills, most of them were for men. They provided popular reading, manuals on the various trades, text-books, and occasionally popular religious works. Educational materials were thus provided for the young people who could not attend school, and apparently they were fairly well used. In some cases, the expenses of the apprentices' library were born by the company or some community philanthropist, but ordinarily they were paid for by small subscriptions from the workers. Most of them were small, but the New York Apprentices' Library reached 50,000 volumes in the first half century after its founding in 1820. In many cases the apprentices libraries were under the control and direction of societies or committees of young workers, and hence their hours of opening and their rules for use were more liberal than those for other libraries of the day.

To about 1850 it can be safely said that the nearest approach to public library service was the social or subscription library. Although privately owned the membership rate was usually low enough for anyone who was likely to be seriously interested in reading. The quantity and quality of reading matter could be, and was, varied to suit the demands of the reading public, and was probably more in tune with popular reading tastes than a public library could have been. At any rate, the social libraries served their purpose for more than a century, and gave way only when truly public library service was achieved. About fifteen per cent of the social libraries founded in New England before 1850 survived into the twentieth century; some of them in their original form, some as public libraries, and some as parts of other collections. But they were not restricted to New England by any means. They spread to the

114

Middle States, and to the Middle West. After 1850, they reached the Pacific Coast, and found popularity in the larger towns there, but in only a relatively few cases were they popular in the South and Southwest.

The circulating library also increased in importance after the Revolution, but its increase was never equal to that of the social library. For one thing, it was restricted, as was the book store of which it was usually a part, to the larger towns. It depended upon a reading public slightly different from that of the social library; more on the casual reader than on the serious student. It was usually small, but in a few cases of old, established stores, it sometimes reached several thousand volumes. Its bookstock was varied, but depended heavily upon fiction and popular biography. Even more than the social library it reflected popular reading tastes, but unfortunately records of circulating libraries are not adequate to show which books were most popular. The circulating library was probably less important than the social library in the ultimate creation of public libraries. On the other hand, it was far removed from the modern drugstore rental shelf, and may be considered more comparable to the public library pay collection.

If we define the public library as being a book collection that is publicly owned, publicly controlled, and for general public use, then there were only a very few public libraries in the United States before 1850. However, those few were important and deserve recognition. In Salisbury, Connecticut, a collection of books donated in 1803 by Caleb Bingham was preserved and made available by the town as the Bingham Library for Youth. It survived to become a part of the present Scoville Memorial Library. In Lexington, Massachusetts, in 1827, the town meeting voted to purchase a library for the youth of the town and to employ a librarian to manage it. The collection was deposited in the town church, but so small was the public support that it went out of existence in 1839. Other examples of small public collections such as these might be found, but the town usually considered as the pioneer in public library service in the United States was Peterborough, New Hampshire. Here, in 1833, it was decided by the town meeting that a part of the State Literary Fund, usually applied to the support of schools, should be used for the purchase of books for a free public library. Other donations added to the size of the book collection, and it was kept for public use in the store that housed the local post office, with the postmaster acting as librarian. By 1837, the collection numbered 465 titles, made up largely of religion, history and biography. The Peterborough Public Library provided a prototype for the future public libraries of the nation. There were a few other tentative beginnings toward public libraries before 1850, but most of our modern public library history starts after that date.

Another type of publicly supported and publicly controlled library before 1850 was the district school library, which originated in New York and rapidly spread throughout the New England and Middle Western states. New York's legislature passed an act in 1835 which made it permissable for school districts to levy taxes for local school libraries. This law brought little response, but a second one in 1838, which provided state funds to match local levies for books, was more successful, and in three years more than 400,000 books were placed in the schools of New York state. This idea grew until by 1850 there were nearly a million and a half volumes in the state's school libraries. Without staff or proper quarters, however, many books were lost or allowed to deteriorate for lack of care. The school library plan was popular at first, and other states followed the example set by New York. In 1837, Massachusetts passed a similar law, and 2084 school libraries were reported by 1850, although they contained all together less than 100,000 volumes. Connecticut followed Massachusetts in 1839, and Rhode Island in 1840, and in this small state at least, the school library system proved rather successful. Several Middle Western states, including Michigan, Indiana and Ohio followed before 1850, but in general their school district libraries were not too successful.

The school libraries were composed of text-books, with a smattering of religious works, of which the majority were above the reading level of children. Several publishing firms took advantage of the school district laws, and hastily compiled sets of works, poorly selected, printed and bound, but sold on commission through local representatives. These sets often took up the entire funds available, and their drab appearance and dry content did little to promote the school library movement. For want of decent quarters, the school library books were often stored in the homes of teachers or school board members, and an investigation of the New York school district libraries in the 1850's found many of the books molding in closets, cellars and attics. Sometimes the teachers opposed the libraries, and even managed to divert the funds for books into salaries instead. But unsuccessful as the school district libraries were, they did serve to establish the precedent of public support for library service.

Much of the secondary education before the Civil War was in the hands of private schools and academies. Their libraries were often poor, but in some cases they approached the level of the smaller college libraries. They often consisted of gift books more than of purchases, and for this reason their contents were not well selected. On the other hand, private libraries of the teachers often augmented the school collection. In the smaller towns of the South and West the academy library was often the best available, and the only one that the average student ever knew.

Along with the other types of libraries that were progressing with difficulty in the early nineteenth century, several important government libraries were established. Of these, the one destined to become the greatest in the western hemisphere was the Library of Congress. The early government of the United States made use of various book collections, but it was not until after the seat of government had been moved to Washington, D.C., that a move was made to create a library for the use of the national officials. In 1800, Congress appropriated the first money for the purchase of books, and in 1802 a room for the library was set aside in the new Capitol building. President Thomas Jefferson appointed the first librarian, who was also the Clerk of the House of Representatives. In its early days, the Library of Congress was almost wholly a legal reference collection for the use of members of Congress, and by 1814, it had only about 3000 volumes. In that year, the Capitol was burned by the invading British Army, and the library was lost. After the war, ex-President Jefferson offered to sell his magnificent private library at cost to the government to replace the lost collection, and after much debate in Congress, the offer was accepted. In 1815, a total of 6700 books were purchased from Jefferson for 23,950 dollars, and this collection made up a library far superior to the one that had burned. Mr. George Watterson was appointed librarian, and temporary quarters for the new library were found in the Post Office Building until 1824, when it was removed to the new Capitol building. By that time, Congress was appropriating 5,000 dollars per year for the national library, and it was growing rapidly in size and importance. At mid-century, the Library of Congress had reached 50,000 volumes, but it was still largely a legislative reference library, and could boast but one librarian and one assistant as its total staff. In 1832, part of the legal works in the library had been separated into a collection for the use of the Supreme Court, but it was still under the jurisdiction of the librarian of Congress. In addition, both the House and Senate had libraries, or at least collections of official documents for their own use.

The various governmental departments also developed libraries of their own almost from the time they were founded. The State Department, for example, had a library built around books of history, international law, diplomacy, and travel, totaling some 3000 volumes by 1825. By 1850, this collection had passed 15,000 volumes, including some 3000 volumes of bound newspapers. From the beginning, the State Department Library collected all the acts and journals of the state and territorial legislatures, and it also developed large collections of foreign public documents. The Treasury Department Library was begun in 1803, but it was not of significant size until after the Civil War. This was also true of the collection in the War Department, although some of the military agencies of the nation such as the Military Academy at West Point, had important libraries. The Academy Library began in 1812 and had some 20,000 volumes by 1850. The Bureau of Ordnance Library began in 1838, and the Artillery School Library

at Fortress Monroe, Virginia, was formed in 1824.
Each of these libraries had about 3000 volumes in 1850.
In the other government libraries there were only small
collections of legal works and government publications,
except in the Patent Office Library which contained
some 20,000 volumes of scientific, historical and legal
works at mid-century.

In addition to the libraries of the Federal government,
most of the states also had libraries in their capitols.
It is quite probable that as early as the Revolution, or
even before, there were collections of legal works a-
vailable in the various legislative halls for the use of
the officers and legislators. Pennsylvania has references to its library in the capitol building in Philadelphia as early as 1777, and New Hampshire claims a
pre-Revolutionary legislative library. However, it was
not until after 1800 that most of the states established
libraries by law, and made definite provisions for their
maintenance and upkeep. South Carolina had a state library as early as 1814, Pennsylvania by 1816, New
York and New Hampshire in 1818, and other states
shortly after. These state libraries were mainly legal
and historical in content, and their acquisitions came
largely from exchange of state publications with other
libraries, and through receipt of Federal documents by
acts of Congress. Gradually the legal works came to
be maintained separately from the historical ones, and
there developed state law libraries or supreme court
libraries in addition to the regular state libraries.
These libraries were, of course, reference libraries for
the most part, except that state officials and legislators
could withdraw books when needed for official use. In
general, these state libraries grew only slowly, and by
1850, all of them together contained only about 200,000
volumes.

The period between the Revolution and the Civil War
saw the development of many important private collections. It was a period when a few fortunes were being
made, and a larger number of business and professional
men were wealthy enough to afford comfortable libraries. The book collections of Presidents Jefferson and
Madison have already been mentioned, and most of the
other Presidents, especially John Quincy Adams, accumu-

lated respectable libraries before or after their terms
in office. Peter Force, the historian, amassed a collection of over 60,000 books, pamphlets and manuscripts,
which his heirs sold to the Library of Congress in 1867
for 100,000 dollars. It forms a most important part of
the historical collections in the national library. George
Ticknor, of Boston, collected over 3000 volumes of Spanish history and literature, which after his death went to
the Boston Public Library. In Philadelphia, Stephen
Colwell, lawyer and economist, bequeathed his library of
some 6000 books and pamphlets on politics and economics to the University of Pennsylvania Library, while
in Cincinnati, W.H. Mussey gave his library of history
and the classics to the Public Library. Elsewhere,
North and South, ministers, educators, merchants and
planters were acquiring notable book collections, a few
of them quite large, but most of them numbering only
a few hundred volumes. Many of these eventually ended
up as parts of public and college libraries, and today
some of the most prized possessions of our larger institutions are books that came from the private libraries
of the nineteenth century.

In the Constitution of the United States, Congress was
given the power to pass copyright laws. Such a law was
passed in 1790, giving any author who was a citizen of
the United States the sole right to print or sell his
copyrighted work for a period of fourteen years, renewable for an additional fourteen year period. In 1831,
this act was replaced by one extending the copyright
period to twenty-eight years, renewable for fourteen
years. In 1846, a deposit law was passed, requiring
that one copy of each copyrighted work should be placed
in the Library of Congress, and one copy in the newly
established Smithsonian Institution Library. The combination of copyright and depository laws promoted the
growth of government libraries.

Another series of laws designed to help the growth of
libraries were those relating to the distribution of public documents. It was understood, of course, that copies
of all federal documents should be placed in the Library
of Congress, and also in all official libraries requiring
them, but in 1813, Congress ordered that copies of all
Congressional journals and documents should be placed

in the libraries of all colleges, universities and historical societies in the United States. During the next
quarter century almost every session of Congress directed that copies of public documents, including census reports and historical works published at government expense, should be distributed to institutional libraries. This aided considerably in building up the
early libraries, and where they have been preserved,
they constitute valuable holdings today. In return, many
of the states passed laws sending copies of their public
documents to the Library of Congress and the State Department Library, and made copies available for exchange with other states. The idea of exchange was
even carried to the international level, and Congress
provided for exchange of United States publications with
other countries.

Bibliography
Bolton, C.K.: American library history. Chicago, 1911.
13 p.
------ Proprietary and subscription libraries. Chicago,
1912. 10 p.
Cole, George W.: Early library development in New
York state. New York, 1927. 19 p.
Conner, Martha: Outline of the history of the develop-
ment of the American public library. Chicago, 1931.
179 p.
Drury, Gertrude: The library and its organization.
New York, 1924. 519 p.
Edwards, Edward: A statistical view of the principal
public libraries of Europe and America. London,
1849. 48 p.
Harris, Thaddeus Mason: A selected catalogue of some of
the most esteemed publications in the English language
proper to form a social library, with an introduction
upon the choice of books. Boston, 1793.
Jefferson, Thomas: Jefferson's ideas on a university
library. Charlottesville, Va., 1950. 49 p.
Jewett, Charles C.: Notices of public libraries in the
United States. Washington, 1851. 207 p.
Joeckel, Carleton B.: The government of the American
public library. Chicago, 1939. 393 p.
Johnston, W.D.: History of the Library of Congress.
Washington, 1904. 535 p.

Keep, Austin B.: History of the New York Society Library. New York, 1908. 607 p.

Lehman-Haupt, Hellmut: The book in America. New York, 1939. 453 p.

Predeek, Albert: A history of libraries in Great Britain and North America. Chicago, 1947. 177 p.

Rhee, William J.: A manual of public libraries, institutes and societies in the United States.. Philadelphia, 1859. 687 p.

Shera, Jesse H.: Foundations of the public library. Chicago, 1949. 308 p.

Shores, Louis: Origins of the American college library, 1638-1800. New York, 1935. 290 p.

Thompson, C.S.: Evolution of the American public library, 1653-1876. Washington, 1952. 287 p.

U.S. Bureau of Education: Public libraries in the United States of America. Washington, 1876. 1187 p.

Carlton, W.N.C.: College libraries in the mid-nineteenth century, Library Journal, XXXII, (1907), 479-486.

Ditzion, Sidney: The district-school library, 1835-1855, Library Quarterly, X, (1940), 545-577.

------ Mechanics and Mercantile Libraries, Library Quarterly, X, (1940), 192-219.

Gilchrist, D.B.: The evolution of college and university libraries, A.L.A. Bulletin, XX, (1926), 293-299.

Stewart, Nathaniel: Sources for a study of American college library history, 1800-1876, Library Quarterly, XIII, (1943), 227-231.

Wellard, J.H.: Popular reading and the origins of the public library in America, Library Journal, LX, (March 1, 1935), 185-187.

X A Period of Library Progress, 1850-1900

Although 1876, with the foundation of the American
Library Association, is often considered the beginning
of the modern library movement in the United States,
the beginnings can be traced to the decade around 1850.
In 1848, Massachusetts passed legislation allowing the
city of Boston to establish a public library and to ap-
propriate municipal funds for its support, thus making
that city the first major municipality in the United
States to have a publicly supported free library. Three
years later this authorization was extended by, "an Act
to authorize Cities and Towns to establish and maintain
Public Libraries." New Hampshire had passed similar
legislation in 1849, and other states followed suit in
later years. It is interesting to note that the New
Hampshire act saw the public library as more than a collection of books, for it authorized the acquisition of
maps, charts, periodicals and other publications as
well as books. In 1850 the national census found no
less than 694 libraries of all types in the United States,
exclusive of school libraries and small private collections. Of these, only five--Yale, Harvard, Philadelphia
Library Company, the Boston Athenaeum, and the Library of Congress--contained more than 50,000 volumes
each.

In 1853 the first national meeting of librarians in
America, met in New York at the call of Charles Coffin Jewett, then the librarian of the Smithsonian Library,
and other interested librarians. Some 82 persons were
in attendance, mostly from the northeast, but including
one representative from New Orleans and another from
San Francisco. Most, but not all, of those present were
active librarians, and they met "for the purpose of con-
ferring together upon the means for advancing the prosperity and usefulness of public libraries, and for the
suggestion and discussion of topics of importance to
book collectors and readers." Among those present were

Seth Hastings Grant, librarian of the New York Mercantile Library; Daniel Coit Gilman, librarian at Yale, and later president of Johns Hopkins University; Reuben Aldridge Guild, librarian at Brown University; and Lloyd Pearsall Smith, librarian of the Philadelphia Library Company. Most of them were outstanding men, and thirty-five of them were included in the Dictionary of American Biography. It is also interesting that almost all of the men present--and they were all men--had some other profession in addition to their library interests and duties. They included ministers, college professors, historians and lawyers, as well as a physician or two and an astronomer.

The topics for discussion at the Conference were mainly subjects familiar to present day librarians. They included cataloging and classification, public reading rooms, circulation of books versus reference use of books, and the question of the distribution of government documents. The best methods of establishing popular libraries throughout the nation was widely discussed, and the need for strong public support for them was pointed out. A central national library, preferably built around the Smithsonian Institution library, was proposed and a committee was formed and given the power to call additional meetings. The time never seemed ripe for such a meeting, and it was not until 1876 that a permanent organization of librarians was formed.

In the last half of the nineteenth century, the growth in number of public libraries was phenomenal. The New England states led the way, and by 1860, Massachusetts reported 45 free public libraries containing over 200,000 volumes. Fifteen years later, despite the Civil War, the same state could boast of 127 libraries receiving at least partial public support and containing nearly a million books. The Middle Western states followed New England in passing laws permitting the establishment of public libraries, and here townships and counties were also given the right to promote library service. This made rural library service possible, and a number of county libraries were established, particularly in Indiana and Ohio. Another development in the promotion of public library service was the establishment of state library commissions. The first library commission was established in Massachusetts in 1890, and by 1900 sixteen other states had formed similar bodies for the aid and support of libraries. For the most part these agencies merely encouraged the establishment of public libraries, advised their personnel, and provided a central clearing house for library and book information. However, in some states, notably in Massachusetts, direct state aid to public libraries was a part of the early library laws, and the disbursing of such aid was directed by the library commission.

A good example of the foundation and growth of a large municipal library can be found in the history of the Boston Public Library. This institution was authorized in 1848, backed up by city ordinances in 1851 and 1852, and finally opened in 1854. Various gifts aided this new library in getting under way. Mayor John P. Bigelow of Boston gave 1,000 dollars, and Edward Everett gave a collection of over a thousand books, including many valuable public documents. Joshua Bates gave an endowment of 50,000 dollars, the proceeds from which could be used for the purchase of books. In 1857, Charles Coffin Jewett came from the Smithsonian Library to head the library, and in 1858, it moved into its own new building. Mr. Bates later gave a large collection of reference works, which together with other volumes was opened in 1861 to the public as the main reference room, or Upper Hall. Under Jewett's direction, printed catalogs of both the circulating library and the reference library were issued, and the library grew rapidly in size and use. By 1875 it contained nearly a hundred thousand volumes and was the most important public library in the nation. Numerous other gifts of money and books, including the Prince Library, collected before 1758, the Bowditch library of mathematics and scientific works, and the George Ticknor collection of Spanish history and literature were added in later years to further the scholarly development of the library.

In contrast to Boston, New York City did not develop a free circulating library until nearly the end of the nineteenth century. But thanks to the generosity of the Astor family, it did have a most valuable public reference library. In 1848, the will of John Jacob Astor provided funds for a free reference library for the city, including the cost of books, building and management. Later his son and grandson added other gifts to form one of the most important libraries in the nation. The Astor library was opened for use in 1854 with 80,000 books, largely the results of buying expeditions made by the first librarian, Dr. Joseph G. Cogswell. By 1875, the Astor library contained over 150,000 volumes, and was rapidly taking its place as one of the most important libraries in the world. Although New York lacked a public circulating library, there were numerous social, society and commercial circulating libraries in operation, making it one of the book centers of the nation.

In the field of college and university libraries, the late nineteenth century was also a period of rapid growth. Many new colleges were established after the Civil War, including colleges for Negroes in the South, state and private institutions in the newly settled West, and the state agricultural and engineering colleges established with federal aid under the Morrill Act of 1862. In the cases of the older colleges and universities, bookstocks increased, departmental and specialized libraries were formed, and trained or experienced librarians were employed. Often literary society libraries became amalgamated with the main library collection, and in a few cases training classes were established for librarians. Harvard University still had the largest college library, and its growth and development during this half century will serve as an example of the other larger university libraries. In 1840, the Harvard library had 40,000 volumes, not including pamphlets; in 1866, there were 70,000 books and 30,000 pamphlets; while in 1875, it owned 150,000 books, nearly as many pamphlets, and with other book collections on the campus it totaled nearly a quarter of a million bound volumes. Harvard's library received numerous gifts in addition to its funds from the college budget. In 1841 it had moved into Gore Hall, a building donated by ex-Governor Christopher Gore, but this was outgrown within a quarter century. It was not until 1913, however, that the new Widener Library was completed, and in the meantime the Harvard Library expanded through various departmental and special collections, as well as in the main library. When this move was made, however, the main library alone

126

contained nearly a million volumes. Other Harvard collections in the late nineteenth century included the Dane
Law School Library of some 25,000 volumes; the Divin-
ity School Library, 17,000; the Medical College Library;
the Museum of Comparative Zoology Library; various
scientific school libraries; and several student society
libraries.

Although school district libraries were widely established in the quarter century after about 1840, they
were not, in general, successful. In 1873, the State
Superintendent of Schools in Wisconsin rather summed
up the viewpoints of his fellow educators when he said
that very few districts were voting sums of money sufficient to build up creditable libraries, and that the
whole system seemed to have come into general dis-
favor, and was more than any other feature of our
school system, the one of which they were least proud.
The situation in Massachusetts was much the same, and
the school libraries there were largely superseded by
free town libraries. In other states where the school
district libraries had been established, the trend was
also toward the public library where experienced personnel could manage the collection. In general, the
school district libraries could be said to have retarded
the general growth of school libraries as we know them
today. There were exceptions, of course, especially in
the secondary schools, and in some of the larger cities.
In Buffalo, New York, for example, in the 1890's the
school libraries were taken over by the public library
which in turn made deposits of selected books in the
various schools during the school terms. These deposits rotated from classroom to classroom, and in the
summers they were returned to the public library for
mending, sorting and general preparations for the coming
year. As more books became available on the child's
level, the public libraries began building up juvenile collections, and by 1900 some of the states were adding
school library supervisors to their state departments of
education. The foundations were laid for the children's
libraries and the school libraries of the twentieth century, but there was still a long way to go.

Among government libraries, the Library of Congress
remained pre-eminent. By mid-century it had reached

some 55,000 volumes in size, but on December 24, 1851, it suffered a disastrous fire, and only 20,000 volumes were saved. These, however, were among the more valuable in the collection, and formed a nucleus from which a new and more permanent library emerged. The library hall in the Capitol wing was rebuilt of fireproof materials, and 75,000 dollars was appropriated by Congress for the replacement of books. By the time of the Civil War it had passed its original high mark and was once more growing rapidly. Prior to 1866 there had been for a time two national libraries. One of these was the library of the Smithsonian Institution, donated to the government by will of the British philanthropist, James Smithson in 1846. Charles Coffin Jewett became librarian of the Smithsonian library in 1847, and proceeded to build it up into a collection of more than 40,000 volumes. He had plans of building it into a real national library, which he felt the Library of Congress was not, and of making it the bibliographical center of the United States. Congress did not agree with him, and in 1866 the Smithsonian library was added to the Library of Congress. The next year Congress appropriated funds for the purchase of the Peter Force collection of early Americana. By 1875, the Library of Congress, still housed in the Capitol building, was approaching 300,000 volumes in size, and had overflowed its quarters.

When Ainsworth R. Spofford became librarian in 1864 the Library entered upon a period of growth and progress. As early as 1871, Dr. Spofford suggested the need for a library building designed solely for the collection, and in 1874 Congress appointed a committee to look into the possibilities for building a national library structure. But the wheels of government grind slowly, and it was not until 1887 that construction began. The building was completed in 1897. This new structure, the present main building of the Library, capable of holding nearly 3,000,000 volumes and covering nearly four acres, was equipped with the latest in library equipment from reading rooms and stacks to book conveyors and inter-office speaking tubes. It was manned by a staff of 185 in 1900, with an additional 45 employees in the copyright office. An immense reclassifying and re-cataloging project had been begun, and this called for a large staff, as did also the new and notable services of printing and distributing catalog cards and providing books and services for the blind.

The other government agencies in Washington continued to develop their specialized departmental libraries. The Department of the Interior Library opened in 1850, that of the Agriculture Department in 1860, and one in the Bureau of Education in 1870. These and the other minor governmental libraries remained relatively small down to 1900, but one of them in particular, the library of the Surgeon-General's Office did attain considerable prominence. Under the librarianship of Dr. John Shaw Billings, an army officer, physician, bibliographer and scholar, this collection grew from a miscellaneous group of some 1800 books in 1865 to a well-organized library of 50,000 volumes and more than 60,000 pamphlets in 1880. Dr. Billings made it one of the best medical collections in the world, developed a subject card catalog for it, began indexing medical journals, and published a bibliography of medical literature. In addition to his many other notable accomplishments, both in the library world and in the fields of public health and hospital architecture, Dr. Billings is to be remembered and honored in the library profession as one of the first and best special librarians.

There were many other specialized libraries that started or improved during this period. In the states, historical, legal and legislative reference libraries were being developed in almost every capital, some adequate in size and scope, others pathetic in their inadequacy. Historical societies throughout the nation were also building up important libraries, with those of the New York Historical Society and the Wisconsin State Historical Society among the best known outside their immediate region. The former of these had 60,000 volumes in 1875, and the latter 33,000. A few specialized medical libraries were emerging, including the New York City Hospital library, with about 10,000 volumes, and that of the Philadelphia College of Physicians, which was about twice as large. Among scientific society libraries, those of the Academy of Natural Sciences at Philadelphia, with about 65,000 books and pamphlets, and the Essex Institute at Salem, Massachusetts, with 30,000 books and

100,000 pamphlets and periodicals, were the largest in 1875. In addition to these there were numerous smaller legal, historical and scientific libraries, ranging from those of county professional societies to the specialized university departmental collections.

The growth of libraries set the stage for the development of a library profession. Although most of the outstanding librarians of this period were members of other professions, they devoted a large portion of their time to library service, developed special skills in that field, and came to consider themselves professional librarians. A few of them were librarians only, including Ainsworth Rand Spofford and Melvil Dewey, and they and others began the systematic training of assistants who in turn became professional librarians. Along with the growth of the profession came the organization of the American Library Association (A.L.A.). The first meeting was held in the hall of the Philadelphia Historical Society, with 104 persons present, including thirteen women. Justin Winsor, the librarian of Boston Public Library and a distinguished historian, was elected president, and Melvil Dewey, then still a young man, was elected secretary. A constitution was drawn up the next year, and the purposes of the association were given as the promotion of public libraries; the encouragement of public interest in, and financial support of, libraries; and the elevation of librarianship to an equal rank with other professions. At the early meetings of the association, papers were presented on very practical subjects: cataloging, indexing, bibliography, book sizes, copyrights, the qualifications of a librarian, and the reading interests of the general public. Growth in membership was slow, but the A.L.A. ranked high professionally, and its meetings called forth speakers of the first rank in the educational field. The needs of different types of librarians were recognized, and in 1889 a section for College and Reference Librarians was formed, with another for Library Trustees following in 1890. By 1900 A.L.A. had nearly a thousand members, representing all types of libraries and nearly every state in the Union.

Closely associated with the A.L.A. and with the library profession in general was the problem of training librarians. Several of the larger public libraries began

training classes for their assistants in the late nineteenth century, but with the exception of the Astor Library in New York City, none of these became a library school. In 1887 Melvil Dewey started a school of
library economy at Columbia University as a regular
part of the university curriculum. Though students
were not lacking, the university administration was far
from enthusiastic about this new development, and in
1889 Dewey took his school of library science with him
when he moved to Albany as librarian of the New York
State Library. There the school prospered and became
a model for succeeding schools. In 1925 it returned to
Columbia University as the School of Library Service.

Two other library training courses were developed be-
for 1900 at technical institutes, one at Drexel Institute
in Philadelphia, and the other at Pratt Institute in
Brooklyn. The only library training course offered at
a state university before 1900 was that at the University of Illinois. For the most part, early training was
very practical, and approached the subject from the
point of view of method rather than theory. Dewey developed a curriculum at Albany which included book
buying, cataloging, classification, card writing, book
lettering, library records, and similar practical subjects. However, Dewey also recommended for future
librarians a sound knowledge of literature, and a general education as well as training in library methods.

Along with the growth of the library profession came
the development of a professional literature. In 1852,
Charles C. Jewett issued from the Smithsonian Library
his Plan for the Construction of Catalogs for Libraries,
with rules and examples. William Frederick Poole,
then at Boston Mercantile Library, began Poole's Index
to Periodical Literature in 1853, as the earliest attempt
to provide a published index to material appearing in
magazines. The first American general work on librarianship was Reuben A. Guild's Librarian's Manual, issued in 1858, which was one of the few concrete results
that came from the Librarian's Conference of 1853. In
1869, Charles A. Cutter, librarian of the Boston Athenaeum, published his Rules for the Printed Dictionary
Catalog, pointing the way toward the dictionary arrangement for library catalogs, rather than the previous

classified subject or topical arrangement. Previous to this decade, library catalogs had almost always been printed in book form, with supplements kept in handwritten sheets or notebooks. About the time that Cutter was formalizing the methods of compiling a printed catalog, Harvard's library was starting the use of handwritten catalog cards, filed alphabetically in trays.

The first edition of Melvil Dewey's Decimal Classification System appeared in 1876, and in the same year the first professional library periodical, the American Library Journal, was begun with Dewey as editor. Before the appearance of Dewey's classification system, every library had its own system, and these varied widely. The new system was simple and practical, and although it did not meet immediate approval, it was gradually adopted. Dewey was not the only librarian to be working on a classification scheme, however, for C. A. Cutter was also developing one, and before he died in 1903 the major part of his Expansive Classification System had been completed. Although it was not widely used in the United States, it did meet with some favor abroad, and in a form greatly revised and adapted, it became the basis for the Library of Congress Classification System, adopted after Herbert Putnam became librarian in 1899. The Library Bureau, a company specializing in library supplies began operating in 1876, and in 1880 the R.R.Bowker Company began publishing the American Catalog of Books in Print. Finally, as the century ended, the Library of Congress began printing its catalog cards and selling them to the libraries of the country, and most of the library services so well known to librarians of the twentieth century had been begun.

Philanthropy was important in the development of library service in the late nineteenth century. Though libraries have always been the recipients of gifts this period was particularly fruitful. One of the first major gifts was Enoch Pratt's endowment of the Free Library in Baltimore in 1886, which under his name and with the later support of the city has become one of the outstanding public libraries in the nation. In the 1890's three large libraries and accompanying funds from the Astor, Tilden and Lenox families were used to form the basis of the New York Public Library. A bequest from

Walter L. Newberry formed the basis of the Newberry Reference Library in Chicago in 1887. The greatest library benefactor, however, was Andrew Carnegie, who began to encourage the construction of free public libraries as early as 1881, and who in about forty years provided financial aid for the construction of no less than 2500 library buildings in the United States, Canada and Great Britain. Hundreds of minor gifts and bequests, to both public and institutional libraries, contributed substantially to the growth of American libraries during this period when public support was still very small.

By the turn of the century, the American library was still having growing pains, but it had passed its infancy and was well on the road to becoming a prominent and necessary part of the American social and cultural scene.

Bibliography

Columbia University: The school of library economy at Columbia College, 1887-1889. New York, 1937. 272 p.

Conner, Martha: Outline of the history of the development of the American public library. Chicago, 1931. 179 p.

Borome, Joseph A.: Charles Coffin Jewett. Chicago, 1951. 173 p.

Cutter, William P.: Charles Ammi Cutter. Chicago, 1931. 67 p.

Danton, Emily M.: Pioneering leaders in librarianship. Chicago, 1953. 202 p.

Ditzion, Sidney: Arsenals of a democratic culture; a social history of the American public library movement in New England and the Middle States from 1850 to 1900. Chicago, 1947. 263 p.

Edwards, Edward: Free town libraries; their function, management and history in Britain, France, Germany, and America. London, 1869. 371 p.

Flexner, Abraham: Daniel Coit Gilman. New York, 1946. 164 p.

Fletcher, W.I.: Public libraries in America. Boston, 1894. 160 p.

Green, Samuel S.: The public library movement in the United States, 1853-1893. Boston, 1913. 336 p.

Hadley, Chalmers: John Cotton Dana. Chicago, 1943.
105 p.

Jewett, Charles C.: Notices of public libraries in the
United States of America. Washington, 1851. 207 p.

Joeckel, Carleton B.: The Government of the American
public library. Chicago, 1935. 393 p.

Johnston, W.D.: History of the Library of Congress.
Washington, 1904. 535 p.

Keep, Austin B.: History of the New York Society Library. New York, 1908. 607 p.

Lydenberg, Harry M.: John Shaw Billings. Chicago,
1924. 95 p.

------ History of the New York Public Library. New
York, 1923. 643 p.

Predeek, Albert: A history of libraries in Great Britain and North America. Chicago, 1947. 177 p.

Rhees, William J.: A Manual of public libraries, institutions and societies in the United States and British
Provinces of North America. Philadelphia, 1859.
687 p.

Rider, Fremont: Melvil Dewey. Chicago, 1949. 151 p.

Shaw, R.K.: Samuel Swett Green. Chicago, 1926. 92 p.

Shera, J.H.: Foundations of the public library. Chicago,
1949. 308 p.

Spencer, Gwladys: The Chicago public library: origins
and backgrounds. Chicago, 1943. 473 p.

Spofford, Ainsworth Rand: A book for all readers...
New York, 1900. 509 p.

Thompson, C.S.: Evolution of the American public library, 1653-1876. Washington, 1952. 287 p.

U.S. Bureau of Education: Public libraries in the United
States of America. Washington, 1876. 1187 p.

Utley, George B.: The librarians' conference of 1853.
Chicago, 1951. 189 p.

Wadlin, H.G.: The Public Library of the City of
Boston, 1911. 256 p.

Wellard, James H.: Book selection, its principles and
practice. London, 1937. 205 p. (includes 70 p. section on "The Historical Background.")

Bishop, W.W.: A decade of library progress in America,
Popular Science, (December, 1904), 131-138.

Carnegie, Andrew: The best fields for philanthropy,
North American Review, CXLIX, (1889), 682-698.

134

Ditzion, Sidney: Social reform, education, and the library, 1850-1900, Library Quarterly, IX, (1939). 156-184.

Fletcher, William I.: The public library movement, Cosmopolitan, XVII, (1894), 99-106.

Harrison, J.L.: The movement for public libraries in the United States, New England Magazine, X, (1894), 709-722.

Johnson, Hazel A.: John Cotton Dana, Library Quarterly, VII, (1937), 50-98.

Mead, Theodore H.: A free lending library for New York; Scribner's Monthly, XX, (1880), 929-935.

Norton, Frank H.: The Astor Library, Galaxy, VII, (1869), 527-537.

Spofford, Ainsworth R.: The public library of the United States, Journal of Social Science, II, (1870), 92-114.

Wright, Thomas: Possible culture through libraries, Contemporary Review, XL, (1881), 25-44.

XI Books and Printing Since 1775

From the days of Gutenberg until the late eighteenth century there were only minor improvements in the printing press and in the processes of printing and binding books. There were improvements in type and illustrations, but printing itself was unchanged. The type was set and inked by hand, the press was raised by means of a turning screw, a sheet of paper was inserted, the press was lowered and the impression made. Each printed sheet meant a laborious raising and lowering of the press and the amount of printing that could be done in a day was very limited. On the other hand, with every step of the process under hand control, very fine work could be done by skilled and conscientious workers.

In 1798, Charles, Earl Stanhope, brought out a press in England that added the power of a lever to the screw process of raising and lowering the press, and this speeded up printing considerably. The Columbian press, an American development about 1810 by George Clymer, did away with the screw press and used levers alone to provide the needed pressure. The Columbian press remained popular for a half century, and was probably the best of the Gutenberg-style flat-bed presses. The great innovation of the early nineteenth century, however, was the rotary press. This machine was first made practical by a German printer in London, one Friedrich Konig, in 1811. By 1814, the august Times of London became the first newspaper to be printed on a rotary press. The rotary press employed a cylinder rather than a flat plate, and could produce a continuous flow of copies. When the rotary press was harnessed to a steam engine, the possibility of making thousands of impressions per hour was finally realized. Along with these new improvements in the press came the use of stereotype plates and cylinders. This process employed movable types to produce solid plates that had the advantage of being permanent and usable for as many impressions as needed.

To the rotary press, stereotypes and steam power, the 1830's saw the addition of the assembly line method of printing, folding, stitching and binding, making possible production of books at much higher speed. In the 1840's the firm of Robert Hoe in New York began producing the Hoe Type Revolving Machine Press, capable of printing 8000 sheets per hour. This type of press was widely adopted for the printing of newspapers and magazines, but many of the older flat bed presses continued in operation for books and fine printing throughout the nineteenth century.

A rival for the stereotype plate came after 1840 in the electrotype plate. Whereas the stereotype plate was made from a papier-maché mold impressed by the original type, the electrotype plate was made by taking an impression in wax from the original type, depositing a thin shell of copper on the wax by an electrolytic process, and then filling in the copper shell with type-metal alloy. Both processes achieved the same result-- a stable plate capable of being continuously used for long runs--but the electrotype plate in the latter half of the nineteenth century gradually displaced the stereotype. The electrotype also had the additional advantage of being able to reproduce pictures from woodcuts or engravings much better than the stereotype.

Despite the improvement in printing methods, type-setting by hand still continued throughout the first half of the nineteenth century. In the 1820's, William Church, a native of Vermont then living in England, designed and constructed a machine for setting type mechanically from a hand-operated keyboard, but the idea was slow to be adopted. It was not until the 1850's that the John F. Trow printing office in New York first put into operation a successful type-setting machine. This machine, patented by William H. Mitchell, was a considerably improved adaptation of the Church machine, and made type-setting a comparatively easy task. On top of this came the production of type-casting machines for the quick and plentiful production of type, both for hand-setting and machine-setting, and the printing trade was rapidly approaching its modern form. One more major printing development came, however, in 1884, when Othmar Mergenthaler built for a New York firm a composing machine, which was patented under the name of Linotype. The Linotype machine was operated from a keyboard, similar to a typewriter, and it cast in one piece a complete line of type, properly spaced and ready for printing or for the making of stereotype or electrotype plates. The Linotype soon took its place as standard equipment in the larger newspaper and book publishing firms.

The new high-speed processes required new strong paper in the form of rolls so that a continuous stream of paper could be fed to the rapidly rotating presses. Above all, this new paper had to be cheap. Up to about 1800, the paper making process, which resulted in flat sheets of good quality rag paper, had been little changed for three hundred years. In 1799, Henry and Sealy Fourdrinier, two brothers who were stationers in London, patented a paper-making machine, and about five years later they produced their first successful working model. This machine was built around a revolving wire band that passed through a vat of paper pulp, picking up a layer of pulp which was then removed from the wires and fed in a continuous stream along a conveyor belt. On this belt the pulp was carried through a process of pressing and drying, producing rolls of paper of almost any needed length. This idea, with some changes, was put into effect in the United States in 1817 by the Gilpin brothers of Delaware. They produced a paper-making machine capable of turning out a continuous sheet of paper, thirty inches wide, at the rate of sixty feet per minute. With many improvements, the Fourdrinier and Gilpin machines remain the basis for most paper-making machinery in modern use. The other great innovation in paper-making in the nineteenth century came in the discovery of new paper-making materials. Linen and cotton rags, the source of paper up through the eighteenth century, were too scarce and expensive for the production of the large quantities of paper needed for the nineteenth century presses. A new, cheaper source of paper was needed, and after much experimentation with various vegetable fibers, a process was developed in the 1850's for making paper from wood

138

pulp. At first the wood was macerated by mechanical means, but soon various chemicals, particularly sodas and sulphites, were used to reduce the solid wood to a liquid, fibrous pulp that could be handled in the paper-making machines. Since there was a seemingly endless supply of wood in the United States, these developments in the making of paper made America the center of the industry for the modern world. So important was the industry, and so rapid its growth, that in 1880 there were 742 mills in 29 states.

Illustrations in American books of the seventeenth and eighteenth centuries were produced either from wood-cuts or copperplate engravings. Excellent work was produced in a few cases, but for the most part, American printers did not equal the Europeans in the quality of their book illustrations before 1800. On the other hand, illustrations were widely used by the American presses after about 1790, and they included not only portraits but maps, architectural drawings, cartoons, prints, and views of the larger cities. Color prints were produced by 1800, and the works of outstanding artists were employed in book illustrations. The American edition of Rees' Encyclopedia, published in Philadelphia in 1797, was a particularly fine example of the copperplate engraver's art. Steel-plate engravings were introduced after 1819, and although the resulting prints were not of the quality of copperplate engravings, the steel could be used almost indefinitely, producing many more copies than copper. Lithography was introduced in the 1820's, and by the 1830's, color lithography was possible. This was the process of reproducing pictures from a flat surface, originally smooth stone, but later zinc or some other metal.

The next great step in book illustration came with the development of photo-mechanical processes, particularly photo-engraving. This process employed chemical means to transfer pictures from the film to the copper-plate, permitting almost any type of photograph to be readily reproduced in print. Photography was common, or fairly so, by 1860, but it was not until 1880 that the first photograph was reproduced in a newspaper, the New York Daily Graphic. The idea spread rapidly to the other metropolitan newspapers, and the photograph soon came to be the mainstay of newspaper illustration. By 1886, the half-tone process was perfected, and this further increased the quality of newspaper pictures. Color printing, rotogravure, and offset printing were all coming into use by 1900, or were well beyond the experimental stages. The latter process is applicable to textual as well as to picture reproduction and whole books are produced by this means.

The final step in the book-making process is the binding, and although the changes have been been so radical, there have nevertheless been many developments in this field in the last century. Before 1800, the sheets of four, eight or twelve leaves were folded, stitched in signatures, then sewn together in volumes, and finally bound in boards covered with leather or vellum. The early printed books simply followed the binding of the later manuscript volumes, and although the bookbinder became an artist in the sixteenth to eighteenth centuries, his artistry lay more in his technique of decorating the leather covers of the book rather than in any departures from earlier book-binding methods. The nineteenth century saw the replacement of leather by cloth as the outside covering, and the wooden or stiff leather boards by heavy paper cardboard. Machine stitching took the place of hand-sewing, and stronger glues were used to strengthen the spine. As the printing presses became more mechanized, and their output more prolific, the process of binding also began to be done by machinery, and by the 1860's, the hand-bound edition was a rarity. The late nineteenth century saw the introduction of wire stapling or stitching for pamphlets and smaller books, and the twentieth introduced the paper-backed, non-sewn, "perfect bound," book that relied entirely upon glue for its binding. In the twentieth century the mechanical processes have virtually replaced hand work, except in setting and controlling the machinery.

One of the results of the change from leather bound books to cloth bindings was the necessity for a protective cover over the cloth to prevent it becoming soiled before the book was sold. This problem found a solution in the paper book jacket, which was first introduced in the 1840's, but which did not come into common use until the last decades of the nineteenth century. The paper jacket or wrapper provided a place for advertising, and for information concerning the book and its author, as well as for attractive illustrations. The design of some book jackets has become an art, but for the most part they remain simply advertising matter. With the coming of the paper-bound books, the jacket merged with the boards of the binding, and resulted in a stiff paper cover, luridly illustrated in several colors.

The nineteenth century publisher was usually a corporation, employing anywhere from a half-dozen to several hundred workers, and often combining under one roof both printing and binding processes. Also, there was a tendency toward specialization, with one press turning out nothing but newspapers, while others specialized in books, magazines or particular types of printing. With the great increase both in the number of presses and their speed, newspapers came out daily, rather than weekly, increased their size and number of pages, and sold by the thousands instead of a few hundred. Magazines increased likewise, from a bare half-dozen around 1800 to several score by 1850, and several hundred by 1900, with some of the more popular ones selling fifty to a hundred thousand copies per issue. Books were also printed in much larger editions, while pamphlets became even more plentiful, and the ubiquitous almanac held its own throughout the nineteenth century.

Whereas much of the early literature printed in the United States was borrowed from European or classical authors, the tendency in the nineteenth century was toward the production of works by American authors. Particularly after 1860, the writers of American birth, whether in literature, history or science, far outnumbered those of European origin in the output of the American press. New types of book publications, including encyclopedias in many volumes, collected works, and the illustrated gift book or annual, entered the field, and the book-seller, long associated with the print-shop, emerged as a separate concern. After about 1840 the publication of text-books for schools and colleges became a major business, as those institutions of learning increased in number and size. Books particularly written and designed for children also appeared in larger numbers, and by the late nineteenth century, the illustrated children's book was an accepted stock in trade for both publisher and bookseller. Shortly after the Civil War the paper-backed novel began to appear in large numbers, and these western, adventure and mystery thrillers made up much of the popular reading of the period.

Among the larger and better known publishers of the early nineteenth century were many names now forgotten, and others that survive in present-day publishing houses. Carey and Lea, for example, headed by the economist and politician, Mathew Carey in the 1810's and 1820's, has come down to the twentieth century as the firm of Lea and Febiger, Inc., of Philadelphia. J. B. Lippincott and Co. was founded in the same city in 1836, and continues to be a major publishing firm today. D. Appleton and Co., founded as a publishing house in New York in 1831, survives in Appleton-Century-Crofts. J. and J. Harper, beginning in 1817, later became Harper and Brothers, and has been for more than a century and a quarter a major publishing firm. By the 1830's Harpers was introducing the assembly line into the printing and binding of books, and employed over 300 workers in one building, a very large undertaking for that time. In the same decade, Harpers began publishing its Family Library, a series of popular books in many subjects, low in price and wide in appeal. It was one of the first of many such series, represented today by the Modern Library and the Home University series.

The Federal Government at first employed various printers, then turned to the appointment of official government printers who received all orders for government printing. This soon became involved in politics, and finally in 1861 when the Government Printing Office was officially opened the government began doing its own publishing.

The publishing industry was not as centralized in the nineteenth century as it became in the twentieth, but the trend toward larger and fewer companies was evident by the 1880's. Thus, in the last few decades, although every town and city had its printing establishments for newspapers and local job printing, most of the books and periodicals were produced in a few large publishing centers.

Many of the larger publishers in the later nineteenth century experimented with the publication of both books and magazines. Harpers, for example, published not only Harper's Monthly, but at different times, Harper's Weekly, Harper's Bazaar, and Harper's Young People. D. Appleton and Co. not only published a periodical, but added the New American Encyclopedia to its list, and for a long time issued a yearly supplemental volume. Charles Scribner and Sons, another pre-Civil War publishing firm, began publishing Scribner's Monthly in 1870 and made of it one of the most important periodicals of its day. But gradually most of the publishers tended to specialize in either books or magazines, and if in books, in particular types of books, such as fiction or science or religious works. By 1872, the publishing industry had its own trade journal in the Publishers' Weekly, although similar but unsuccessful works had been tried as early as 1852. Several attempts at a catalog of all books published in the United States were tried, but the first successful one to be continued for any time was the American Catalog, begun by Frederick Leypoldt in 1880. It covered the years from 1876 to 1910, and provided an index of books in print. As such it became a standard tool for both the book-trade and the librarian. It was replaced in the early twentieth century by the H.W. Wilson Company's United States Catalog, and its companion, the Cumulative Book Index.

From a few scattered printers in the thirteen colonies of 1775, the American publishing industry of the 1950's has become a gigantic business, employing thousands of workers and producing millions of volumes per year. Mechanical, electrical and chemical progress has greatly changed the printing processes, and now the world of electronics has opened even wider the field of communications. Not only does radio and television compete with and enlarge the older means of transferring and preserving ideas, but they provide instantaneous communication--something undreamed of in 1775. If there was a public demand for it, it would be perfectly possible to develop a radio-newspaper that for the price of a television set would produce newspapers in the home

143

direct from central news rooms in New York or Washington. Yet, despite all changes, the book and its kindred materials are still basically the same as the first papyrus roll of hieroglyphics--they are media of communication, preserving knowledge for days, months or centuries, and transmitting it.

Bibliography

Aldis, Harry G.: The printed book. Cambridge, England, 1951. 3rd. ed., 141 p.

Bennett, Paul A.: Books and printing. New York, 1951. 258 p.

Davenport, Cyril: The book, its history and development. New York, 1930. 258 p.

Green, Ralph: The iron hand press in America. Rowayton, Conn., 1948. 40 p.

Hunter, Dard: Papermaking: the history and technique of an ancient craft. New York, 1947. 680 p.

Jackson, Holbrook: The printing of books. London, 1938. 285 p.

Lehmann-Haupt, Hellmut: The book in America. New York, 1939. 453 p.

McMurtrie, Douglas C.: The book. New York, 1943. 676 p.

Marinaccio, Anthony: Exploring the graphic arts. Scranton, Pa., 1946. 275 p.

Miller, William: The book industry. New York, 1949. 156 p.

Morison, Stanley: Four centuries of fine printing. London, 1924. 243 p.

Nicholson, Margaret: A manual of copyright practice. New York, 1945. 255 p.

Pitz, Henry C.: A treasury of American book illustration. New York, 1947. 128 p.

Pottinger, David: Printers and printing. Cambridge, Mass., 1941. 143 p.

Reiner, Imre: Modern and historical typography. New York, 1946. 125 p.

Rosner, C.: Printers progress, 1851-1951. Cambridge, Mass. 1951. 119 p.

Simon, Howard: Five hundred years of art in illustration. New York, 1942. 476 p.

Simon, Oliver: Introduction to typography. Cambridge, Mass., 1945. 137 p.

Weeks, Lyman H.: A history of paper manufacturing in the United States, 1690-1916. New York, 1916. 352 p.

Weitenkampf, Frank: The illustrated book. Cambridge, Mass., 1938. 314 p.

Wroth, Lawrence C.: A history of the printed book. New York, 1938. 507 p.

- - - - - - -

Kalijarvi, Thorsten: International copyright protection, U.S. Department of State Bulletin, XXX, (April 5, 1954) 530-534.

Rawley, James A.: An early history of the international copyright movement, Library Quarterly, XI, (1941), 200-206.

Ransom, Will: Five hundred years of printing, Publishers' Weekly, CXXXVI, (August 5, 1939), 381-384.

Printing--Ancient craft is stirring with technological innovations, Fortune, XL, (October, 1949), 100-109.

Hagedorn, Leo H.M.: The first century of photo-engraving, Penrose's Annual, XIX, (1917), 189-197.

McMurtrie, Douglas C.: The printing press moves westward, Minnesota History, XV, (1934), 1-25.

Morison, Stanley: Towards an ideal type, The Fleuron, II, (1924), 57-75.

Rollins, Carl P.: A survey of the making of books in recent years, The Dolphin, I, (1933), 288-301.

XII Modern Foreign Libraries

As one might expect, library service in Canada, our nearest neighbor, has developed in much the same way that it has in the U.S. Public library service in Canada dates from the Free Libraries Act, passed in 1882. While the School Libraries Act, passed in 1848, came earlier it was generally ineffective before 1900. One of the most important libraries in Canada is the Library of Parliament, in Ottawa, with its 500,000 volumes, and its outstanding collection of Canadian law and history. Each of the provinces has a provincial library, with the largest being that of Quebec, and there are several large public libraries, especially those of Toronto (800,000 volumes), Montreal, Winnipeg and Vancouver. University libraries of importance include those of Laval University at Quebec, which has the largest French language collection in Canada, McGill University at Montreal, the University of Toronto, and the University of British Columbia at Vancouver. Province-wide library service is most effective in Ontario, but the western provinces are improving their libraries through traveling collections and regional libraries. Package libraries are available from several of the provincial libraries for the benefit of inhabitants who live far from the centers of population. The only approved library schools are those at McGill University, and the University of Toronto but many Canadian librarians have received their library training at American institutions. Canadian librarians have been active members of the American Library Association, and their standards of library service and librarianship are as high as those of the United States.

The library picture in our southern neighbor, Mexico, is not as favorable as that in Canada. The National Library in Mexico City, which numbers some 300,000 volumes not counting pamphlets and manuscripts, is considered one of the best in Latin America. It was first opened to the public in 1869, and numbers among its treasures more than 100,000 manuscripts relating to the history and development of the nation. Since 1920, the development of public library service has been encouraged by the government and there are today some 5000 public libraries in Mexico, but most of them are very small. In addition to these public libraries there are several large libraries in the nations's colleges and universities, and a few of the larger churches have small but historically valuable collections. The Benjamin Franklin Library in Mexico City a joint Mexico-U.S. venture, provides books in both Spanish and English for all readers.

The situation in Mexico is duplicated more or less throughout all Latin American countries. In almost all of them there is a national library of some size, but few public or institutional libraries of note. Library service is hampered by the generally poor educational facilities and by low economic status of the majority of the population.

In recent years, Brazil, Argentina, Chile and Cuba have taken the lead among the countries of South America in the field of library service. Brazil in particular has several outstanding libraries, and reported in 1949 a total of 127 federal libraries, 133 provincial libraries, 445 city libraries, 1592 libraries in educational and cultural institutions, and 477 special libraries. These 2774 libraries contained, altogether, nearly eight million volumes. The National Library at Rio de Janeiro contains nearly a million volumes and some 200,000 manuscripts. This library also contains the Brazilian copyright office, and operates a school of librarianship. In Sao Paulo the municipal library, which contains nearly a quarter million volumes, is housed in a building that towers twenty-four stories high and cost over a million dollars. It, and other larger libraries in Brazil, are thoroughly modern in organization and management. Brazil has also taken a lead in library extension, and has developed bookmobile services in some of its rural and frontier areas. In Sao Paulo for example, there is in addition to the public library a bookmobile library service for suburban areas, and a large free library especially for children. In Rio de Janeiro, there is a National Catalog

Exchange Service which provides centralized cataloging and printed catalog cards for subscribing libraries all over the nation. There is also a national union catalog in process of formation at the Getulio Vargas Foundation Library.

In Argentina, the largest and most important library is the National Library at Buenos Aires, with its more than half million volumes and some 50,000 manuscripts. It was founded in 1810, and contains some of the rarest historical materials in any of the Latin American libraries. In 1946, the Argentine government reported a total of 1508 public and institutional libraries in the country, with roughly 5,000,000 volumes serving as many registered readers. It should be pointed out, however, that these figures include all school libraries and school children, who, at least theoretically, have library service available to them through the National School Library Service. The library of the National University at Buenos Aires numbers some 275,000 volumes, and several other colleges and universities have sizeable collections. There is a school of library science in Buenos Aires, a national library association, several regional library associations, and even a national department of public libraries.

The National library of Chile has some half million volumes, and in 1950 that country reported 327 other public and private institutional libraries. With the exception of 21 city libraries, all public libraries in the nation are under the direction of the National Library Service. There is a school for librarians at Santiago, and a national association of librarians. The University of Chile at Santiago has a main library and 22 departmental libraries, containing in all more than four hundred thousand volumes.

In Peru, the National Library was burned in 1943, but it was re-opened in 1947 and is growing rapidly. Peru has, in the library of the San Marcos National University, what is probably the oldest library in the western hemisphere. It was founded before 1600, possibly as early as 1575. Venezuela has a National Library of some 200,000 volumes, as does also Uruguay, and there are modern municipal libraries in such cities as Caracas

148

and Montevideo. But outside of the national capitals and major cities, library service in the remaining South American countries has been very slow in developing. Some of the West Indian Islands have good library systems, and Cuba in particular has an excellent national library of over a quarter million volumes.

The West European countries have, as one might expect from history, some of the largest and most important libraries in the world. In England the most important single collection is that of the British Museum. It is one of the largest libraries in the world, with more than five million volumes. Its holdings in many fields, ranging from Anglo-Saxon manuscripts to Egyptian papyri, are among the best in the world. Other great English libraries include those at Oxford and Cambridge Universities, the former with nearly three million volumes and the latter with better than two million. The universities at Edinburgh, Manchester, Liverpool, Aberdeen and London all have libraries containing around half million volumes each. There are in London a number of government and special libraries, many of them quite large and containing valuable collections. One interesting special library, a subscription library surviving from the pre-public library days, is the London Library, with over a half million volumes available only to subscribers; many of these subscribers live in distant parts of England, and borrow books by mail.

Though a few of England's public libraries date from earlier periods, the public library movement has largely developed since the 1870's. In 1950, there were no less than 587 central libraries in England, Scotland, Wales and Northern Ireland, containing over 42,000,000 books and serving 12,000,000 readers through some 23,000 service points. These are supplemented for research purposes by more than 10,000,000 volumes in college and university libraries. As an example of a large English public library, the City Library of Manchester has 33 branches, a staff of 350, and an annual circulation of 6,500,000.

The British Library Association was formed in 1877, and today it has more than 10,000 members. The libraries of England suffered great losses during World War II from the enemy bombing raids. The British Museum lost a wing which housed some 150,000 books and 30,000 bound volumes of newspapers, many of them not duplicated elsewhere. Many smaller public and college libraries suffered partial or complete destruction, and the total book loss of the war, including libraries, bookstores and publishers' warehouses, was estimated at no less than 20,000,000 volumes. Since 1945, British library service has concentrated on replacing war losses, on extending library service to rural areas, and on improving library service to working people, particularly through trade union reading clubs and factory library deposits.

In France the great national library, the Bibliothèque Nationale, is another of the world's great cultural institutions. Having developed over a period of some 500 years, it has received books by virtually every possible means, including gift, purchase, copyright law, expropriation and military conquest. The Bibliothèque Nationale was modernized considerably during the nineteenth century. Scholars and students are allowed to use it with some restrictions. Its bookstock today is over five million, besides hundreds of thousands of manuscripts, a half million maps and plans, and valuable collections of stamps, prints and paintings. The libraries of the University of Paris have collections totaling more than a million and a half volumes, and there are no less than thirty-three other college and institutional libraries of notable size in Paris alone. Also, there are numerous special and government libraries, including the Bibliothèque Ste. Genevieve, a historical library of some 800,000 volumes; the library of the National Assembly, with more than 400,000 volumes; and the combined libraries of the French Institute (including those of the French Academy and the famous Bibliothèque Mazarine), with more than 1,500,000 volumes. Counting all school, government, special, institutional and large private collections, there were no less than 1100 libraries in Paris in 1950.

Outside of Paris there are many other important university and municipal libraries. The universities at Grenoble, Bordeaux, Lille, Lyon and Toulouse, to name but a few of the largest, have collections numbering from one to five hundred thousand. In addition to books, these libraries often have large collections of manuscripts, some dating back for several centuries. The large cities, such as Marseilles, Lyons, and Bordeaux have magnificent libraries, some of them founded centuries ago, which contain hundreds of thousands of books, but on the other hand, many smaller towns and villages have no public libraries, and little or no access to library service. Since the early 1900's, when a national library survey was made and a library association was formed, considerable effort has been made by the national and departmental governments to extend library service to all citizens of France. In 1945 a library division was set up in the Ministry of Education to coordinate and improve library service to all parts of the nation.

In the nineteenth century Germany was probably the most advanced nation in the world in library service. Not only in the size of its book collections and in the numbers of its libraries, but in its library methods and general librarianship it was far ahead of both England and the United States. The outstanding municipal and university libraries of the world patterned themselves after the German libraries, to about 1875. Prior to World War II, the major German libraries were the National Library in Berlin, with 1,500,000 volumes, including one of the largest collections of incunabula in the world; the State Library of Bavaria at Munich, almost as large; and the State Libraries at Dresden and Stuttgart, both over a half million volumes. University libraries at Bonn, Breslau, Gottingen and Freiburg contained approximately a half million volumes each, and there were others equally important. German municipal libraries, particularly in the larger cities, had better research collections than most American colleges, and in addition to these there were literally thousands of village and small town popular libraries, the Peoples Libraries or Volksbibliotheken.

When the Nazis came to power in Germany the growth of libraries was seriously curtailed, except for a few favored institutions. All public libraries were placed under strict state control, and censorship over their contents was maintained. Many books were restricted from circulation, and library service was considerably hampered. The military action of World War II destroyed many German libraries, damaged others, and hundreds of thousands of volumes, including rare books and manuscripts, were lost. Since 1945, however, the libraries of Western Germany have been rebuilt, and aid in gifts of books and funds has been provided from the United States in many cases.

In Eastern Germany, under Communist domination, books and libraries are controlled by the government. Under the pretense of removing pro-Nazi books from the public and institutional libraries a general housecleaning of all books unacceptable to the Communist commanders was made, and thousands of volumes were destroyed or confiscated. In their place Russian and pro-Communist works were substituted, and their reading was made practically compulsory. Many private and instituional libraries were expropriated by the Russians on one pretext or another and either taken to Russia or turned over to the new workers' libraries. At Potsdam, outside Berlin, a new Communist university was opened, and its library was made to conform to the new political philosophy. Throughout East Germany, books and libraries are considered a definite part of the propaganda war. Libraries and librarians are closely controlled, and there is little or no freedom of speech or press. What has happened to the great public and university libraries of Prussia and Silesia is not definitely known, but it is certain that some of the rarer and more valuable works were carried eastward by the conquering Russian armies in 1945.

In Italy the library situation in the twentieth century has been somewhat similar to that in Germany. As of 1900, some of the finest libraries in the world were in Italy, but two World Wars and two decades of dictatorship have taken their toll, and although not as much physical damage was done to Italian libraries as to the German ones, the deterioration due to lack of proper care has been almost as destructive. Although the larger reference and research libraries of Italy contain some of the most valuable materials in the world, popular library service has not been widely developed, and public libraries as we know them in the United States did not exist in most towns and cities prior to World War II.

Of all the libraries in Italy, the Vatican library is the most outstanding. In 1926-1927, the Carnegie Corporation sent William Warner Bishop, to survey the problems of the Vatican Library and make recommendations for its future growth and development. Dr. Bishop's recommendations led to the new addition, the modern book stacks, the re-organization program, and the general redefining of the purposes and aims of the library. It now has a depository catalog of the United States Library of Congress printed cards, and thus serves as a bibliographic center for all of Italy.

The major public libraries of Italy are all controlled by the National Library Service, including the two National Central Libraries at Rome and Florence, and thirty other state libraries, many of them formerly important private or ecclesiastical libraries. In 1875, the majority of the monastery libraries in Italy were taken over by the government, and these formed the basis for the present state library system. The National Central Library at Florence is the largest library in Italy, but the Victor Emanuel National Library in Rome is almost as large. There are several large university libraries in Italy; among them are Bologna, Naples, Padua and Palermo. A few of the large privately endowed libraries have survived into the twentieth century, with the Biblioteca Casanatense at Rome containing over 400,000 volumes in literature, religion, law, economics, social sciences and history. The Biblioteca Ambrosiana at Milan, developed from a private library founded in 1609, now has over half million volumes, plus many manuscripts, including holographs of Petrarch and Leonardo da Vinci. A number of specialized government libraries in Rome round out the Italian library scene, but despite the notable large libraries, there is still a need for smaller, popular reading collections, adapted to the needs of the average citizen rather than designed for the scholar. Since World War II, steps have been taken in this direction, and public reading rooms have been established in industrial areas and in the smaller towns. The Communists have also made use of this idea and have opened reading rooms filled with Communist propaganda in the larger cities.

Elsewhere in Europe, the development of library service has in general followed one of two patterns. In Belgium, Switzerland, the Netherlands and the Scandinavian countries, library service has followed the German system, with strong state libraries and many small popular libraries. Denmark has probably the best public library service of any country in Europe. The Royal Library in Copenhagen has over a million volumes and it is only one of several large government libraries. Outside of the capital city a system of public libraries and library stations brings books to virtually every citizen of the country.

In the southern parts of Europe, including Spain, Portugal and the Balkans, a second pattern of library development has been followed. This area also has a few large libraries, but it has failed to back them up with a public library system. The Spanish National Library at Madrid, for example, has a million and a half volumes, and there are a few other large libraries in Barcelona and Madrid, but outside these metropolitan centers there are very few, even in educational institutions, of over a few thousand volumes.

In the Balkans, the Greek National Library at Athens has some 600,000 books and pamphlets, and national libraries in the other countries number more than a hundred thousand volumes each, but public library service outside of the larger cities is virtually non-existent.

In Eastern Europe, behind the Iron Curtain, library service is strictly controlled by the governments and is part of the propaganda system. Russia claims to have the largest library in the world in the Leningrad Public Library (the Lenin State Library), the largest number of libraries of any country in the world, and the largest number of library books in use. The Leningrad Public Library, formerly the Russian Imperial Library, began from books captured in Poland in the 18th century. Since the Soviet revolution it has been increased in size considerably by confiscations of private collections and

absorbing smaller government and church libraries. Today it claims to have over fourteen million volumes.
Another large Russian library is the V.I. Lenin Memorial Library in Moscow with more than five million volumes, and there are several other government libraries in Moscow and Leningrad which own a hundred
thousand or more volumes. State libraries in Kiev and
Minsk have over a million books each, and each of the
other provincial capitals has a large national library.
In addition to these reference libraries, there is a national system of public libraries based on municipal,
regional and district collections all over the Soviet Union. Fantastic numbers of books and figures for circulation are reported from these institutions. The latest
figures give a total of 86,000 public libraries in Russia,
holding more than 166,000,000 volumes. In all, including school, factory and collective farm book stations,
there are claimed to be more than 250,000 library service outlets, or one for every 800 Russians. There are
library schools at the larger Russian universities, and
library training classes in many of the larger libraries.
Several library and bibliographic journals are published,
and there are national and regional library associations.
There was great destruction to libraries in the parts of
Russia overrun by the Germans in World War II, but
much of this destruction had been rebuilt by 1950.

Practically speaking, there are no private libraries,
behind the iron curtain, although a few prominent officials do have sizeable book collections in their homes
or offices. The Russian librarian must also be a propaganda expert, politically conscious, socially active, and
a trained speaker. He must take the library services
to the people, rather than waiting for them to come to
his library. The Communists have used the book as a
powerful weapon.

Many Polish libraries were destroyed during World
War II, but according to reports in 1950, library re-
construction was well on its way. At that time the Polish Minister of Education reported 22,000 public libraries and books stations, and 24,000 school libraries, all
centrally controlled through a system of regional, county
and village libraries. Librarians are trained in the
universities, and also in the larger public libraries. The

Polish National Library has branches in both Cracow and Warsaw, and these along with the University of Warsaw Library are the largest in the nation, each having around a half million volumes.

Rumania under the Communists has all libraries controlled by the government, in divisions of government libraries, school libraries, army libraries, research libraries, and public libraries. Over 11,000 public and village libraries were reported in 1952, along with an additional 6000 factory and trade union libraries. The Rumanian librarian is described as an enthusiastic partisan on the ideological front, and an active Communist worker. As in other Communist countries, Rumania makes full use of the radio in library and book review programs.

Czechoslovakian libraries are not so completely controlled, but they are nevertheless under Communist domination. The research libraries at Prague, after having been censored for anti-Communist books, were thrown open to the public, as were the old and famous university libraries at Olmutz, Brunn and Pressburg. In Hungary, similar treatment was received at the half-million volume National Library in Budapest, and in the library of the University of Budapest. In theory, this opening of the university and research libraries to the general public sounds good, but actually, with insufficient staffs it has meant that the student and research worker has suffered while the general reader has gained little that he could not have received at the public libraries. Bulgarian libraries are considerably behind those of other East European countries, but progress is reported there in governmental libraries, school libraries, and service to rural and factory workers.

Elsewhere in the world, with a few exceptions, library service is far behind that in Europe and America. Australia and New Zealand have good systems, including large public and university libraries. In Australia the public libraries are under state rather than national control, and each of the Australian states has a large central library. The national library at Canberra, founded in 1927, is not as large as some of the state, municipal and university libraries. The state libraries of New

South Wales at Sydney, (600,000 volumes), and of Victoria at Melbourne (700,000 volumes) are the largest in Australia, with the libraries of the Universities of Sydney and Melbourne being almost as large. In New Zealand, public and school libraries are under national control, and since 1945, the National Library Service has endeavored to reach every citizen in the country. The Public Library at Auckland has about 300,000 volumes, while that at Wellington is somewhat over half as large. A system of town and village libraries covers both of the major islands, and for New Zealanders living outside of towns, rural traveling libraries and parcel post book packages are available. In South Africa there are excellent public libraries in Johannesburg and Capetown, and several large university libraries as well. The Johannesburg Public Library has half a million volumes, with branches, school and hospital deposit libraries, and bookmobile service. There is a South African Library Association, a library periodical, and a library school at Capetown. Library service for the most part, however, is for the two million white people of South Africa, and service to the eight million natives is limited.

In the Philippines, libraries suffered considerably during World War II, with an estimated 95 percent of all library books in the city of Manilla being destroyed. Since 1945, aid from the United States has helped in the rebuilding of Philippine libraries, and considerable progress is being made. Under the new Philippine Republic, a National Library will be built in Manila that is hoped to be one of the finest in the Orient. There is a government bureau of public libraries to promote library service throughout the islands. In Japan, prior to 1945, there were a few large university libraries, and the Imperial Library in Tokyo numbered about a half million volumes, but library service in general was not comparable to that in the West. Since that date a library mission from the United States has studied the library problems of Japan, and recommended a system of public, school and college libraries under general government control but with considerable local autonomy. A library school has been established in Tokyo and courses for school librarians are available in other colleges. The former Imperial Library is now a part of the National Diet Library, which in all of its departments contains about a million and a half volumes.

Library history in China is nearly as ancient as that
nation itself, for the Chinese have always respected
learning. At the beginning of the Christian era there
was a library of 11,000 volumes in China, and its catalog in book form has been preserved. But modern
China, partly because of wars and economic troubles,
has not had a chance to develop a widespread library
system. In the 1920's, which was about as peaceful a
decade as the Chinese have witnessed in the twentieth
century, some progress in library service was made,
with the development of several large university libraries, and over 500 public libraries. The National Library in Peking contains some two million volumes,
with large numbers of manuscript works and examples
of early Chinese printing. The new Communist government in China has set up a Bureau of Libraries in its
Department of Cultural Affairs, and undoubtedly it will
make full use of books and all other means of communication in its attempt to control the minds of its people.

In India, where the British were in power for more
than two centuries, the larger cities have municipal libraries, and there are a number of fairly adequate college and university libraries. But due to the many different languages and the low economic status of the majority of the Hindu people, there has been little general
library development. Since the independence of India,
there have been established in some of the states, particularly in Baroda and Indore, a system of state-wide
library service. In the past two decades, a few Indian
educational leaders have urged the creation of public
and school libraries, and particularly since 1947, much
progress has been made. An Indian Library Association
has been formed, and this group is encouraging library
development and publishing library literature in several
languages for the nation's librarians. S.R. Ranganathan,
a leading Hindu librarian, recently retired, has written
widely on library science. He is among many strong
sponsors of a new National Central Library for India,
built along the general plan of the Library of Congress.

In the Moslem countries, from Pakistan to Morocco,
there are a few fine old libraries, many of them con-

taining priceless manuscripts, but there are a few really modern institutions. Turkey has been developing a library system along modern lines since 1927, when by law the Latin alphabet was adopted for the Turkish language instead of the Arabic alphabet. Egypt has a modern public library in Cairo, and several large university libraries. In Syria, Lebanon and Iraq modern libraries are being established in the capital cities, and a few colleges have libraries along western lines, but for the most part, free library service for the people is lacking. The new Jewish state of Israel is very library conscious, and is establishing public, school and government libraries as rapidly as its economic condition will permit.

In the world at large, a bright hope on the library scene comes from the United Nations Educational, Scientific and Cultural Organization. Its general thesis is that since war begins in the minds of men, it is in the minds of men that war must be prevented. Free libraries are a great weapon in fighting the prejudices, falsehoods and fears that lead to wars, and for this reason UNESCO is doing everything it can to promote library development all over the world.

Bibliography

Bostwick, Arthur E., ed.: Popular libraries of the world. Chicago, 1933. 316 p.

Burton, Margaret: Famous libraries of the world; their history, collections, and administrations. London, 1937. 458 p.

Carnovsky, Leon, ed.: International aspects of librarianship. Chicago, 1954. 132 p.

Esdaile, Arundell, ed.: National libraries of the world; their history, administration and public services. London, 1934. 386 p.

Hirsch, Rudolf, ed.: Changing patterns of scholarship and the future of research libraries. Philadelphia, 1951. 133 p.

Kenyon, Frederic: Libraries and museums. London, 1930. 79 p.

Library association of China: Libraries in China. Peiping, 1929. 43 p.

McColvin, L.R.: The public library system of Great Britain. London, 1941. 218 p.

Munn, Ralph: Australian libraries, a survey. Melbourne 1935. 139 p.

------ New Zealand libraries. Christchurch, 1934. 68 p.

Newcombe, Luxmoore: The university and college libraries of Great Britain and Ireland. London, 1927. 220 p.

Orcutt, William: The magic of the book. Boston, 1930. 315 p. (See pp. 63-104: "The resurrection of the Vatican Library".)

Ranganathan, S.R.: Library tour, 1948: Europe and America: impressions and reflections. Delhi, 1950. 219 p.

------ Library development plan for India. Delhi, 1950. 462 p.

Richardson, E.C.: Some aspects of international library cooperation. Yardley, Pa., 1928. 168 p.

Rivera, Rodolfo: Preliminary list of libraries in the other American republics. Washington, 1942. 181 p.

UNESCO: The development of public libraries in Latin America. Paris, 1953. 192 p.

XIII Modern American Libraries

Library services have made tremendous progress in twentieth century America, and the public library in particular has become widely known and used.

The public library that was to become the largest of all in the United States was formed only a few years before 1900. This was the New York Public Library, finally brought together into one unit in 1895. The Astor Library, a public reference collection, had been in the possession of the city since 1848, and had been open to scholars a few hours daily since that time. Since 1870, the Lenox Library, a smaller but somewhat more popular reference library donated by James Lenox, had also been available. Neither of these libraries loaned books for outside reading. In 1879 a Free Circulating Library was formed, with partial public support, and by 1895 this institution had eleven branches. In addition, there were literally dozens of other libraries in New York, semi-public in nature, but receiving little or no public assistance, and being supported almost entirely by charitable or professional organizations. In 1886 Samuel Tilden left the bulk of his estate, including his own collection of some 20,000 volumes to the Tilden Trust, with the power to found a free public library in New York City. When the Tilden funds became available in the 1890's, the city fathers of New York decided to combine all their libraries into one centrally controlled system. This was done in 1895, the New York Public Library was created, and Dr. John Shaw Billings was appointed as the first Chief Librarian. At first there was no central library and the Tilden collection was housed in the Astor building, while the Lenox Library remained in its own quarters. In 1901, Andrew Carnegie, donated 5,200,000 dollars to the city of New York for the erection of 65 branch libraries, and these were erected in the next few years. A movement for a centrally located main library building had been under way since 1897, but it was not until 1911 that this was completed and opened to the public. This building, now known as the New York Public Library, is mainly a reference library, housing the Lenox, Astor, Tilden and other research collections. By 1913, the entire system contained over two million books and pamphlets, and circulated more than 8,000,000 items to 343,000 registered borrowers. Its annual budget had already passed a million dollars, and it was rapidly becoming one of the most important libraries in the nation.

The Chicago public library originated in 1873, not long after the disastrous Chicago fire of 1871, and opened its doors with a collection of some 3000 books. It grew rapidly with important gifts from local citizens, from the East, and even from England. William Frederick Poole, already noted for his periodical index begun at Boston, and for his successful librarianship at Cincinnati Public Library, became the first librarian at Chicago. Temporary quarters were used at first, but by 1876, the library was located in a new building, contained 48,000 volumes, and was serving 23,000 registered borrowers. Its growth was rapid, and by 1913, its 600,000 bookstock was made available to the public by a staff of 238 employees. Today its more than two million volumes make it one of the largest public libraries in the world, and its position in the cultural life of its city is outstanding.

The coming of the First World War slowed down the development of public library service somewhat, but it did bring about another event in library history that had a lasting effect. This was the formation of libraries for the use of service men in camps, on ships, and overseas. Over 1,600,000 dollars was raised by public subscription to finance this venture, and its direction was placed in the hands of the American Library Association and the American Red Cross. With the A.L.A.-A.R.C. books thus purchased, or donated by libraries and individuals, 47 major camp libraries, staffed by trained librarians, were set up at training bases and overseas headquarters. In addition to these, 261 smaller libraries and over 2500 supply points, deposits of 50 to 100 books each, were placed at smaller posts, on board ships, and at Red Cross canteens. These books were well used, and there can be little doubt that many soldiers and sailors who became acquainted with books during their service career, came home with an increased interest in reading and libraries. At any rate, the return of peace and relative prosperity in the 1920's saw many smaller towns opening their first public libraries, while the larger, firmly established libraries extended their services, acquired new buildings, and explored new fields of librarianship. Library extension, in particular, came into its own during the post-war decade, and county libraries in many parts of the nation moved out of the experimental stage. State library commissions were active, but public funds for library service remained small, and trained and experienced help was still scarce.

The depression years that began in 1929 at first brought severe difficulties for public libraries. Budgets were reduced and services were curtailed. But under the Works Progress Administration new library buildings were completed and additional library workers were secured. In some cases new branches were opened and staffed, bookmobiles were sent into rural areas, and books were mended and periodicals bound. The W.P.A. library program in many states offered state-wide library services, bringing books to areas where libraries had never before been known, and when this program was discontinued local government agencies continued library aid. The Tennessee Valley Authority began a regional library experiment in seven states, and brought public library service to many counties that had hitherto had none. From New England to California, the development of rural library service improved considerably, and 3,000,000 more Americans had library service in 1939 than in 1934. Still, nearly a third of all Americans were without libraries, and only 400 of some 3000 counties were offering county-wide library service. In addition to the Federal aid through the temporary agencies, several states began to provide direct aid for public library service, particularly in rural areas.

The effects of the depression years, both favorable and unfavorable, can be seen in the U.S. Office of Education's public library statistics for 1938-1939. The number of libraries had increased to 6880, and they con-

163

tained more than 104 million volumes. Some 24 million registered borrowers in the year 1938 had taken home over 400 million volumes, and more than 7 million new books had been added to public library shelves during that one year. The Northeastern and Middle Western states still had the largest number of libraries, but the remainder of the nation was increasing its library service at a rapid rate.

In the South there was rapid growth in many of the larger city libraries, and also a wide increase in the number of rural county or regional libraries. Throughout the nation, the number of trained and experienced librarians had increased steadily during the depression years, and as of 1938, nearly 16,000 full or partly trained personnel were serving in public libraries full time, and an additional 5000, with similar training, were working part-time.

Between the depression years and the mid-twentieth century came the long years of the Second World War. Unlike the First World War, however, this world conflict did not greatly hamper the development of public library service, and indeed tended to encourage it. There were shortages of personnel in many cases, and in some war industry areas the rapid growth in population resulted in restricted library service. The services rendered by the public libraries to the nation went far beyond the usual educational and recreational reading matter. In maintaining public morale, in serving business and industry, and in the broad field of adult education and public information, the wartime services of libraries can hardly be underestimated. Without exaggeration it can be said that America's public libraries more than proved their worth to the nation during the trying days of World War II.

After the war the public libraries saw a rapid return to normal conditions, and then a progressive surge ahead with new branches, new buildings, and new services offered to the public. New problems arose with television and the millions of paper-backed reprints that flooded the book market. Postwar shifts in population added thousands of patrons to some libraries and subtracted them from others. Two groups in particular--

164

those under twenty-one and those over sixty-five--
increased out of proportion to the remainder of the population, and they provided a ready and willing public
for the library's services. But in the main, those problems have been met, and the public library is the
stronger because of them. Television has been wel-
comed as an ally, and even as a tool for library service. The paper-backed thriller relieves the public library of part of its task in supplying purely entertain-
ment reading. The population changes have been met
with improved services to children, special library departments for teen-agers, and also for the sixty-fivers.
With more libraries, more books, more staff, and with
full use of all modern developments, the American public library at mid-century was forging ahead, stronger
than ever. There was still nearly one-fifth of the nation without public library service, but that fraction
was annually growing smaller.

College and university libraries have also progressed
rapidly since 1900. The average college library of
that date was small, and consisted almost entirely of
the classics and contemporary textbooks. It was staffed
with only one or two librarians, was little used by the
students, and was usually housed in a room or wing of
the college administration or classroom building. With
the exception of a half-dozen major universities, the
concept of the college library as a research center was
almost entirely absent. The idea of the college library
as a storehouse of knowledge, where books were preserved rather than used, was still common, and the concept of the librarian as a curator of a repository of
ancient tomes was still prevalent.

Harvard University Library had, by 1900, been surpassed in size by the Library of Congress, but it was
still by far the largest university library in the nation.
Its bookstock then numbered 560,000, including the main
library and all departmental and special libraries on
the campus, and it was far ahead of Yale with its
285,000 volumes, and the University of Chicago with its
329,000. Other major university libraries at the turn
of the century included those at Princeton, University of
Michigan, Cornell, Johns Hopkins, Dartmouth, University
of California, and the University of Pennsylvania. Har-

vard moved into the new Widener Library in 1915. The Widener Library was designed to fill the library needs of the University for an indefinite period, but subsequent years have seen it supplemented by the Houghton Library for rare books and manuscripts, the Lamont Library for undergraduates, and no less than seventy other departmental and associated libraries on the campus.

On other university campuses, the library scene in the early 20th century was much the same as that at Harvard, although in most cases it was on a much smaller scale. New buildings were erected, staff was increased, and book budgets were brought into line with the growth in number of students and faculty. This was the period when the college library ceased being a museum and became a teaching center. Newer teaching methods called for more student use of the library, and more faculty interest in book selection. The seminar method of teaching especially placed great emphasis on the use and proximity of books. Growing graduate schools demanded rare and expensive books and periodicals for research. Above all, the increasing size of libraries meant that books and materials had to be better organized and arranged, so that in many cases whole libraries had to be re-cataloged, with new classification systems employed. Fortunately, this was also a period of library philanthropy, when most of the major universities, and many minor ones, received substantial gifts in money, buildings and books. The 1920's saw a number of university libraries in the South and West beginning to compete in size and importance with the older ones of the Northeast. The libraries of the technical and agricultural institutions were not equal in size, but their significance in their own fields was becoming recognized, and the fact that the library was as much a necessity as the laboratory was generally accepted. On many campuses there was conflict between those who wanted all books in a central library, and those who preferred departmental collections. In general, the latter group won, and in a few cases where a new building brought everything together for a short time, the demands of the faculty and departmental heads soon brought the re-establishment of the special subject libraries. As the donations of books and funds for library purposes became smaller, many universities and colleges turned

to the formation of Friends of the Library groups,
where many could make small gifts which would take
the place of a few large ones.

With the coming of the depression decade college and
university libraries were as hard hit as the public libraries. Staffs and budgets were curtailed, and plans
for expansion and improvements were often shelved indefinitely. Once again, the coming of the N.Y.A. and
W.P.A. programs brought temporary relief and some
colleges were able to go ahead with binding, cataloging,
indexing and other long delayed projects. In the case
of public institutions, Federal relief funds were sometimes available for aid in constructing library buildings.

In order to extend the services which their budgets
could not provide, university libraries experimented with
cooperative buying programs, in which neighboring collections shared expensive materials, or coordinated
their buying of rarer works. Union catalogs and inter-
library loans furthered this cooperation, and photo-mechanical means of reproducing printed materials were
widely used. By the time the effects of the depression
began to wear off, World War II came with all its problems. During the war years, funds were usually plentiful, but staff problems increased, and the demand on
campus libraries multiplied by the needs of military
training programs, newly organized departments, and
war information centers. Under the pressure of need,
however, new methods of library service were employed,
new tools were developed, thousands of new workers
were introduced to the library field, and the end of the
war saw the nation's college and university libraries
stronger than ever. Everywhere academic libraries
were taking stock of their assets, accomplishments and
aims, and were planning for sound and useful service
in the postwar years.

The postwar years saw rapid expansion for the nation's colleges, and their libraries kept up. Thousands
of veterans flooded the campuses, and both undergraduate
and graduate enrollments rose. Hard put at first to
meet this demand, the libraries soon adjusted, and once
again went into a program of new buildings, annexes and
departmental collections. By 1953, Harvard's total book

collection was nearing six million volumes, while that at Yale had passed four million. Ten other university libraries had passed the million mark, and the collection of half million volumes was becoming almost a norm. Five universities had library budgets of over a million dollars annually, while fifteen had staffs of more than a hundred members each.

The school library as we know it today is almost entirely a twentieth century development. There were, to be sure, school libraries in New York and New England even before 1850, but they were really book deposits, unorganized and uncataloged, with little supervision. At the turn of the century, many educators and school administrators were thinking in terms of public library service to the schools. Many public libraries were building collections of books for children, and inviting school children and teachers to make use of them. In only a few cases were there deposits of books in the schools, and the concept of the school library as a separate unit with its own trained librarian was not generally accepted. In 1896, the National Education Association formed its school library section, and in the same year a joint N.E.A.-A.L.A. committee began working on the problem of library service to children, both in and out of school. The next year, a special conference of the American Library Association was held in Atlantic City to discuss the relationship of libraries and schools.

In the next decade, however, changes in the philosophy of elementary and secondary education decided the question in favor of the library in the school--or at least in favor of books in the school. The introduction of such new ideas as the platoon school, the Winnetka plan and the Dalton plan, all involving the development of initiative on the part of the child, called for books at hand at all times. The idea of developing and educating the child through freedom rather than compulsion, made the use of books, both for instruction and for pleasure reading, a necessity in the new methods of classroom teaching.

By 1910, the standard goal of schools was a library of at least one thousand volumes, supervised by a librarian or teacher-librarian, and under the general direction of the school principal and superintendent.

The library report of the United States Office of Education for 1899-1900 would seem to indicate a rather large number of school libraries in operation at that date, but is misleading. To be sure, no less than 3189 schools in the nation reported having school libraries, and of these 1725 reported more than a thousand books each, but few of these, if any, were libraries in the current sense of the word. A description of the average secondary school library in 1913 which would be even more applicable to those of 1900, said "Secondary school libraries are weighed down with books long since out of date, or with antiquated books... Most of them are small collections of reference and text books, poorly quartered, unclassified, and neither catalogued or readily accessible for constant use."

By 1913, the nation's schools reported 3265 libraries of over 1000 volumes. What was more significant, 607 of these libraries reported full-time librarians, and altogether the reporting schools possessed more than 6,000,000 volumes. Most of these books and libraries however, were in the Northeast and Middle West, and in the larger cities. Most of the metropolitan areas had school library systems by this time, with regular service from a headquarters library to the numerous public schools in an entire urban area.

In 1935, the most complete statistics ever gathered on the nation's school libraries were compiled, and 27,724 schools reported a total of more than 28,000,000 volumes, for an average of 1017 volumes each. Of these libraries, however, only 3808 reported full-time librarians, and another 8770 part-time librarians.

Credit for the growth in school libraries during the twentieth century belongs to several groups, most important of which were the National Education Association and the American Library Association. Both of these organizations encouraged the development of school libraries, the training of librarians, and the establishment of school library standards. In addition to various N.E.A. divisions and committees concerned with school libraries, the National Council of Teachers of English in 1914 appointed a standing committee on school libraries, and the A.L.A. in the same year established its School Library Section. N.E.A.'s Committee on Library Organization and Equipment in 1920 published its pamphlet on Standard Library Organization and Equipment for Secondary Schools, giving librarians and school administrators a goal toward which they could aim their library development. This report received the endorsement of the American Library Association as well, and provided standards of size and contents for junior and senior high schools of various enrollments. In 1925, the N.E.A. Department of Elementary School Principals followed with its Elementary School Library Standards, also approved and republished by the A.L.A. In addition to these, state departments of education, state education and library associations, and library schools also made surveys, studies and reports that added to the sum total of information available on school library services and standards.

Aside from standards and statistics, however, there were other significant developments in school libraries. The development of state aid for school salaries and library books, the certification of school librarians, and the growing interest of school administrators in the school library are all indications of the progress that was being made. Charitable foundations, such as the General Education Board and the Rosenwald Fund gave financial aid to school library demonstration projects in various parts of the nation, particularly in those areas where school library service had lagged behind. For example, in 1929, the Rosenwald Fund provided aid for eleven county library systems to demonstrate public library service to both Negro and white rural schools. The Carnegie Corporation's aid to library schools also furthered the development of school libraries. The trend toward cooperation between public and school libraries has been noticeable since the 1930's, with a few cases of centralized buying and processing for all publicly owned books and materials within a given city or county. One other favorable trend is the increasing amount of research done on the school library. Both library schools and teachers colleges have encouraged research in this field, and such research adds valuable material to the amount of information available on the subject.

Although statistics can indicate the tremendous growth in school libraries between 1900 and 1950, they do not tell the whole story. This story lies in the growth of the numbers of books available for children, in the improvement of types of children's books, in the extension of library service, and in the new methods of bringing books and children together. To understand all this, one must be able to visualize the various types of libraries serving school children, the varieties of materials available for them and the qualifications of the teachers and librarians who serve them.

There is a wide range in types of school libraries. The large high school library may consist of a suite of rooms, including reference room, browsing room, periodical room, conference room, and work room. Its staff will probably include two or three trained librarians in addition to clerical help, and its available materials will be made up of books, pamphlets, pictures, slides, films, film-strips, maps and recordings. It may have an audio-visual aids room adjoining it, where projection equipment, record players, radio and television receivers will be available. Its field of service will include all the graphic arts, whether book or non-book, its annual budget may run into twenty or thirty thousand dollars, and its collection may be ten thousand or so books and several thousand other items. In contrast, another school library may consist of only a few hundred books, shelved in a study hall, uncataloged, and available for use in the room only. Between these extremes lies what we might call the average high school library.

The average high school library has about 3000 volumes, with a full-time librarian who has had at least partial library training. The library consists of only one room, equipped with standard library furniture, but probably used as a study hall during some periods. The books are cataloged, and the standard reference materials, including dictionaries, encyclopedias, and magazine indexes are available. About thirty or forty periodicals are received regularly, and at least some of these are bound or preserved in storage. No clerical help is

available, except for unpaid student assistants, and the
librarian is kept more than busy with the numerous duties in the library, plus a few non-library ones. She
is well aware of additional service which she could
render in the way of audio-visual aids, public relations,
and teaching the use of the library, but she simply
does not have the time for them. She finds her greatest service in individual work with the students, and
she feels most gratified when a book, whether new or
dog-eared, comes to rest in the hands of an eager
reader.

In addition to the centralized high school library,
there are several other types of school library services.
There may be a high school with specialized subject
collections in the various classrooms, and no central
library at all. Then there is the elementary school library, with centralized or classroom collections or
both. The centralized elementary school library will
resemble the high school library, except that the furniture will be smaller, the books will be selected for the
younger readers, and the atmosphere will probably be
a little less formal. Many school library authorities
recommend the classroom collection for the first three
grades, with an introduction to a centralized library
coming in the fourth to seventh grades. Sometimes
there is a combined elementary and junior high school
library, a combined junior-senior high, or a combined
senior high and junior college library. The separate
junior high school with its centralized library is also
becoming common. The old problem of classroom versus centralized library seems to have been resolved in
favor of the latter, but there are still many advocates
of books in the classroom, and the result is sometimes
a compromise in which standard reference works are
permanently located in each classroom, and collections
of books for general reading are rotated between rooms
from time to time from the central library.

In addition to grouping of school libraries by functions
or by types of students served, there is also a wide division among them from the administrative point of
view. The school library may be directly under the
school principal or superintendent, and have no relation
to any other library. On the other hand, it may be part

172

of a school library system, such as a city school organization, an independent school district, or a county school system. In either case, the individual school library is a part of a larger organization; with many advantages and possibly a few disadvantages over the independent library. In a school library system, book purchasing and processing is usually done centrally. In such a system, there may be one or more high schools, plus many elementary schools; a few trained librarians, and many teacher librarians. Each school gets to use many more books in the course of a year, but has less voice in their selection. There are advantages in economy also, but some critics hold that the school library system merely postpones the day when each school will have its own library, and that it is a makeshift rather than a solution to the school library problem.

In some cases the public library in the city or county serves all schools; the purchasing and processing is done by the central library and books are placed on deposit, either in school libraries, or directly in the individual classrooms. Other variations in school library organization include the public library adjacent to the school and serving as a school library, or the public library which has a branch in the school building. Professional libraries for teachers may be a part of the school library, or may be kept separately or in a central teachers' library open to all school personnel in an entire district, city or county. Libraries for parents, not exactly public libraries, but collections of books on education, child psychology and the like, are being tried in a few schools.

Paralleling the growth of public, college and school libraries in the twentieth century has been the rapid development of special libraries, particularly those of the Federal government. The realization that necessary books and source materials should be at hand for all government agencies has led to the establishment of a number of libraries not only in Washington, but at regional headquarters throughout the nation.

The Library of Congress is the nation's greatest library, and two others serve as national libraries: the Department of Agriculture Library, with about a million volumes and the Armed Forces Medical Library, which is almost as large. The various Departments and agencies all have libraries, some of which are large and important. Each of these libraries is designed to serve a particular purpose, but at the same time, all are available to the general public in one way or another. Government libraries have not been confined to Washington. Many major departments of the Federal government have branches or regional offices scattered throughout the nation. Libraries are maintained in many branch offices. Some agencies, like the Tennessee Valley Authority, have developed notable libraries at their headquarters. TVA's main library at Knoxville quickly grew in the 1930's to some 30,000 volumes, plus many thousands of pamphlets, films and other materials. In addition, TVA maintained popular and technical libraries at its major construction projects, and encouraged the development of public, county and regional libraries throughout the Tennessee valley area. More recently the establishment of the Atomic Energy Commission, with major branches in Tennessee, Washington, Illinois and South Carolina, has brought the development of major research libraries at each location.

Besides its major libraries in various offices in Washington, the Department of Defense, through its Air, Army and Navy branches, has libraries literally all around the world. There are large libraries at West Point Military Academy, at the Naval Academy at Annapolis, and at the newly formed Air University in Alabama. All permanent military and naval bases have large popular and professional libraries, as do all the service hospitals. The larger naval vessels have libraries on board, and the smaller ones have rotating collections made available through the Navy Department's Library Services Branch. Bases overseas, whether in Okinawa, Europe or North Africa, all have their own libraries, varying in size according to the number of personnel, and according to the services rendered. This supplying of popular and educational reading materials for men and women in uniform has been a most important stimulant to reading and self-education during and since the war.

During the war a new type of library service was

introduced overseas. This was the United States Information Library which was designed to inform foreign readers about America and its way of life. Thousands of books in English and native languages were stocked in these libraries, and their effect on eager readers was a wholesome supplement to our international diplomacy.

In addition to its own libraries, the Federal Government has been interested in the general development of library service of all types throughout the nation. Since its founding in the nineteenth century, the Office of Education has provided valuable service by collecting and publishing statistics about libraries, and has also published advisory material for librarians, particularly on the school level. In 1938, a Library Service Division was established in the Office of Education, with consultants for both school and public libraries. These specialists prepared booklists and manuals, and also made themselves available for talks to library association meetings, to other professional groups interested in library service and for advice to libraries. In the 1930's the President's Advisory Commission on Education suggested Congressional legislation to provide federal aid through state agencies for both school and public libraries, primarily in the more sparsely populated rural areas. The idea behind this was the need for equalization of school and library services throughout the nation--to make schools and libraries as good in one part of the United States as in another.

Not to be ignored in a discussion of government libraries are those of the states. These state libraries, although usually devoted primarily to history or law or both, have in many instances grown into important reference and research collections. The state libraries usually serve as reference libraries, but in most cases their books are available to citizens of the state through mail or interlibrary loans. In some cases, the state library also serves to promote and encourage the development of library service. In addition to those libraries designated as "state libraries," most states also have special collections such as Supreme Court libraries, or legislative reference libraries, and some state departments, such as those for education or agriculture

may have sizable libraries of their own. In many
cases, the best collections of public documents in the
state can be found in the library of the secretary of
state. State archival agencies, really specialized manuscript libraries, are sometimes connected with the
state library, and sometimes maintained as separate
organizations.

In a general sense, government libraries are all special libraries--that is, their collections are specialized,
or their function, or reading public, or all three are
specialized. However, the libraries most generally considered as special libraries are those of professional
associations, technical schools or departments of universities, public institutions such as hospitals and prisons, and those of business corporations. These libraries, many of which are quite large, serve only a limited clientele, but are considered so important to that
small number that they often have large staffs. Outstanding among the special libraries are the endowed
libraries, often semi-public in nature, such as the Newberry and Crerar libraries in Chicago, the Folger
Shakespeare Library in Washington, and the Huntington
Library in California. The John Crerar Library was
developed from funds given by a Scotch immigrant who
had made millions in industry and banking. It is a
technical and scientific reference library of over a half
million volumes. The Newberry Library, endowed by
Walter L. Newberry also in Chicago and almost as
large as the Crerar Library, is a reference collection
devoted to literature, history, philosophy and music.
Both of these libraries are open to the public for reference use. In San Marino, California, the Huntington
Library and Art Gallery is largely a rare book collection, but as such it is one of the finest in the nation,
with collections that are not duplicated elsewhere. In
Washington, D.C., the Folger Shakespeare Library is
an endowed institution, devoted to material by and about
William Shakespeare, the theater and the era in which
he lived. The Pierpont Morgan Library in New York
City, is another endowed reference library, strong in
incunabula, history and early Americana. One of the
most recently established of these research libraries
is the Linda Hall Library, of Kansas City, Missouri,
which is devoted largely to science and technology.

These and other such collections in other cities and on college campuses throughout the nation are usually open to serious students although almost all are strictly reference libraries and some have other restrictions as to use.

Almost as valuable as the endowed libraries are those of the historical societies throughout the nation. Many of these had their beginnings in the nineteenth century or earlier, and their holdings are very important. The Wisconsin State Historical Library in Madison is one of the best historical libraries in the world. Other important historical society collections include those of New York, Minnesota, Illinois and Massachusetts. Many similar society libraries, such as the Boston Athenaeum, or the Grolier Club Library in New York are also of great research value. In addition to the historical societies, many scientific organizations have libraries noteworthy for their size and contents. The New York Academy of Medicine library has nearly 200,000 volumes, plus an additional 100,000 pamphlets, and the Engineering Societies Library in the same city is nearly as large. In Philadelphia, the Academy of Natural Sciences Library and the American Philosophical Society Library are noted for their reference and research collections, and throughout the country there are hundreds of technical, scientific, legal and religious society libraries ranging in size from a few hundred to several hundred thousand volumes. They make a very great contribution to the total research resources of the country.

In the past half century or so, another type of special library has appeared on the American scene. This is the business or technical library of the large corporation. Consisting of highly specialized books, periodicals and pamphlets, these libraries are ordinarily used by the personnel of the particular company, but they are usually available to other serious students. Banks, insurance companies and large newspapers were among the first businesses to realize the importance of having their own reference libraries, but industrial firms were soon to follow. The New York Times has a library of over 25,000 volumes, backed up by information files containing more than a million items. The Standard and Poor's Corporation of New York has a library of

177

some 40,000 volumes on business, finance and industry, Other companies have libraries ranging from a few hundred volumes up, and many of them are staffed by trained librarians and used by constantly growing numbers of company researchers. The DuPont Company, for example, has libraries at each of its major industrial plants, in addition to one of about 20,000 volumes at its headquarters in Wilmington, Delaware. Most of the large chemical, steel, automobile, oil and mining corporations have their technical libraries. Smaller special libraries, popular in nature, are the libraries in hospitals, prisons and other public welfare institutions. These are usually small, but their collections change rapidly to keep up with the demands for current popular literature.

The special library field has grown tremendously in the decades since World War I. The number of trained librarians entering this field has increased steadily, and to meet their needs the Special Libraries Association was formed. A survey of special libraries in the United States was published in four volumes in 1941-1947 under the title of Special Library Resources. It is one of the fullest accounts of any one type of library available, and it indicates beyond question the economic, cultural and even military value of special libraries to the nation.

Bibliography

American Library Association: College and university library service. Chicago, 1938. 159 p.
------ College and university libraries and librarianship. Chicago, 1946. 152 p.
------ A national plan for public library service. Chicago, 1948, 168 p.
------ School libraries for today and tomorrow, functions and standards. Chicago, 1945. 43 p.
-------A survey of libraries in the United States. Chicago, 1926. 4 vols.
Asheim, Lester, ed.: Forum on the public library inquiry. New York, 1951, 281 p.
Bostwick, Arthur E.: The American public library. New York, 1929. 471 p.
Branscomb, B.H.: Teaching with books. Chicago, 1940. 258 p.

Brough, Kenneth: Scholars' workshop; evolving conceptions of library service. Urbana, 1953. 197 p.

Cecil, H.L.: School library service in the United States, an interpretative survey. New York, 1940. 334 p.

Henne, Frances: Youth, communication and libraries. Chicago, 1949. 233 p.

Jackson, Lucille, ed.: Technical libraries, their organization and management. New York, 1951. 202 p.

Joeckel, Carleton C.: The government of the American public library. Chicago, 1935. 393 p.

Johnson, Alvin: The public library, a people's university. New York, 1938. 85 p.

Johnson, B. Lamar: Vitalizing the college library. Chicago, 1939. 122 p.

Leigh, Robert D.: The public library in the United States. New York, 1950. 273 p.

Lydenberg, Harry M.: History of the New York Public Library. New York, 1932. 643 p.

Lyle, Guy R.: The administration of the college library. Chicago, 1939. 122 p.

Manley, Marian C.: The special library profession and what it offers. New York, 1938. 132 p.

Moshier, L. Marion: The small public library: organization, administration, service. Chicago, 1942. 143 p.

Rider, Fremont: The scholar and the future of the research library. New York, 1944. 236 p.

Salamanca, Lucy: Fortress of freedom. Philadelphia, 1942. 445 p. (A popular history of the Library of Congress.)

Schenck, Gretchen K.: County and regional library development. Chicago, 1954. 272 p.

Walraven, Margaret K.: Teaching through the elementary school library. New York, 1948. 183 p.

Wilson, Louis R.: The geography of reading. Chicago, 1938. 481 p.

------ The university library. Chicago, 1945. 570 p.

XIV The Growth of the Profession of Librarianship

A profession is usually characterized by having (a) a body of specialized knowledge, (b) advanced facilities for specialized education, and (c) a professional association to improve services and to increase the quality and quantity of services and of professional personnel.

Professional tools
The growth of libraries in the modern era has been closely paralleled by the development of those bibliographic and technical aids without which library service could hardly function. Classification manuals, subject heading guides, bibliographies, indexes and textbooks in library methods all aid the librarian in serving the reading public, and the story of the development of library literature and the librarian's tools is a part of the history of libraries.

It has already been noted that 1876, the year so important in American library history, saw the beginning of the Library Journal and the first edition of Melvil Dewey's Decimal Classification System. These useful library aids were followed in 1880 by the first volume of Frederick Leypoldt's American Catalog, the first record of books in print in the United States. Previous catalogs of Americana had appeared, of course, and the Publishers' Weekly had attempted since 1872 to keep up with the current output of American publications. The American Catalog continued to appear at intervals until 1910, but before that date it had been superseded by the H.W. Wilson Company's United States Catalog, and its periodical supplement, the Cumulative Book Index. The latest one volume edition of the United States Catalog, that of 1928, listed more than 190,000 titles. The Cumulative Book Index keeps this national bibliography up to date, and provides an author, subject and title index to books and pamphlets published in the United States or elsewhere in the English language. Another exhaustive bibliographic tool is the **R.R.** Bowker Company's Publishers' Trade List Annual, which is a compilation of all available publishers' catalogs for a given year, bound together, and in recent years indexed by author and title in a separate volume entitled Books in Print.

The Dewey Decimal Classification System went through several editions before 1900 and by that date it had been widely adopted by public, school and college libraries throughout the nation. As the new editions grew longer and more complex, an abridged edition was issued for the use of smaller libraries. But the development of the Library of Congress Classification System provided a more suitable system for the classification of large libraries. Many of the larger university and technical libraries turned to this system during the early twentieth century, and the Library of Congress aided them by publishing the L.C. classification in frequently revised and expanded editions. To supplement the classification guides came the A.L.A. Catalog Rules of 1908, and Subject Headings for Use in Dictionary Catalogs. Just as important to the average library was the service provided by the Library of Congress in preparing and selling printed catalog cards. These cards, available after 1901, provided full author information, title, collation, L.C. classification number, and suggested subject headings. In later years the Dewey classification number has been added. L.C. cards are available for most American publications and many foreign ones, and have gradually been expanded to include all cataloged books in the Library of Congress. The average library can now purchase cards for virtually all books added to its collection. The Library of Congress also publishes its own Guide to Subject Headings, and other bibliographic aids for the use of its own staff and other librarians who care to purchase them.

The early twentieth century saw a number of new aids available for the interested librarian. Possibly the most used book selection tool was the A.L.A. Catalog, first published in 1893. In 1904, this catalog included 8000 titles, suitable for use in a public library, and it formed a standard and guide for the use of all small libraries. This was continued by new editions and supplements to 1949. Another useful aid in book selection the Book Review Digest, began to appear in 1905. It provided a brief summary of several reviews for each of hundreds of the more popular and important books published each year, and these reviews aided the librarian in deciding which of several possible books to purchase. Serving as an index to book review literature, as well as a selected subject guide to new books, the Book Review Digest has proved to be a most important library tool. Since it suggests Dewey class numbers and subject headings it also serves as a cataloging aid for the smaller library. Even more selective in approach is the H.W. Wilson Company's Standard Catalog Series. This series began with the Children's Catalog in 1909, when for the first time an extensive but selective bibliography of current children's literature was made available. The Children's Catalog was followed by the Standard Catalog for Public Libraries in 1918, and the High School Catalog in 1926. Each of these aids provides a classified selection of the latest books in each field, with a dictionary catalog of authors, titles and subjects. There are brief annotations, and some collections are analyzed to provide further information for the librarian. Classification numbers and subject headings make these tools indispensable, with the result that they are basic purchases for libraries in their respective fields. Along with other Wilson publications, they appear in a cumulative form, with a basic volume about every five years, kept up to date by semiannual and annual supplements.

The aids already mentioned are only a small part of the library service program provided by the H.W. Wilson Company. In the field of periodical indexing, Poole's Index to Periodical Literature, begun in 1853, was about the only thing available before 1900. There had been other attempts at general periodical indexing, but none was successful. Even Poole's Index was hardly satisfactory, since it was very selective, difficult to use, inaccurate in places, and rather erratic in its publication. After many tribulations, it ceased publication in the early 1890's. Several attempts at a successor failed, and finally in 1901, H.W. Wilson took over the task and began the publication of the Readers' Guide to Periodical Literature. This succeeded, after some difficulties, largely because the Wilson Company adopted the custom of charging for its publications according to the value of each to a particular library. This service basis of prices enabled smaller libraries to obtain the Wilson publications at lower prices, and hence their use was widespread. Another feature of the Wilson publications is the system of cumulative issues, and cumulative indexes, that reduces the number of places to look for a particular bit of information.

The next Wilson index after the Readers' Guide was the International Index to Periodicals, begun in 1907. This index, started as a supplement to the Readers' Guide, indexed a selected list of some 175 periodicals in the humanities and pure sciences, largely of a scholarly or scientific nature. These were not received in the smaller school and public libraries, and did not need to be included in the Readers' Guide, but they were needed in the larger libraries. The need for special indexing in another field was met in 1908 with the Index to Legal Periodicals, and other subject fields have been covered by the Industrial Arts Index, begun in 1913, the Agricultural Index (1916), the Art Index, (1929), the Education Index (1929), Library Literature (1936), and the Bibliographic Index (1938). Current Biography, a collection of sketches of currently important people, was begun in 1940, and this was supplemented in 1946 by the Biography Index, which lists biographical material appearing in some 1500 periodicals, plus numerous collected biographies and pamphlets. Other important Wilson library aids include the Essay and General Literature Index, started in 1931, which indexes books of essays and collected articles in all fields; the Fiction Catalog (1908), the Abridged Readers' Guide (1935), the Educational Film Guide (1936), the Catalog of Reprints in Series (1940), and the Filmstrip Guide, (1948). The Union List of Serials, begun in 1927, contains about 120,000 serial titles and indicates the holdings in these titles for some 650 large libraries. This was compiled with the aid of an American Library Association committee, and was revised in a 1943 edition with later supplements. The Vertifical File Service, begun in 1932, is an annotated subject index and buying guide to pamphlets.

Aside from its indexes, the H.W. Wilson Company

also provides other reference aids, including; the Reference shelf, and the University Debaters Annual. In 1938, Wilson added to its already impressive list of library services the production of printed library catalog cards. These cards, available currently for several thousand of the more popular adult and children's books, are simpler in form than the Library of Congress cards, and are less expensive. They are available either with or without printed call numbers and subject headings. The Wilson cards meet the need of the small public and school libraries for catalog cards, and provide what amounts to a centralized, subscription cataloging service.

Not the least important of the Wilson publications are the several hundred books and pamphlets on the subject of library service and library history, and the dozens of study guides and bibliographies and their periodical, The Wilson Library Bulletin.

The R.R. Bowker and Company began in the 1870's to issue the Publishers' Weekly, a current index to books and pamphlets appearing in the United States. This is a most complete source of information concerning current and forthcoming books. Early in its history, the Bowker company took over the publication of the Library Journal, which had been begun by A.L.A., and has published it since as one of the most generally useful library periodicals. Regular features of the Library Journal include selected and annotated lists of new books; news about librarians and about library associations. The Bowker Company also publishes the American Library Directory, a guide to the location, personnel and resources of libraries, large and small, all over the United States and Canada, and Ulrich's Periodicals Directory, which lists periodicals of all types and all countries. Many important books for the library and book-trade professions have appeared under the Bowker imprint.

The American Library Association also is a major publisher of library tools. These include the Booklist and the Subscription Books Bulletin, both designed to aid the librarian in the wise selection of books, and the A.L.A. Bulletin, which is the professional journal of the association. The Booklist is a selected and annotated list of current books suitable for purchase by the average small library, while the Subscription Books Bulletin is a critical guide to new reference works, particularly those that are sold by subscription. The Bulletin provides news of the Association's activities, publishes articles of general library interest, and serves as a sounding board for discussion of current library problems. Since 1904 A.L.A. has published a Guide to Reference Books, first edited by Alice B. Kroeger, then by Isadore G. Mudge, and now by Constance M. Winchell. This is the standard textbook for students in reference classes, and a guide for all reference librarians. A List of Subject Headings for Use in Dictionary Catalogs was compiled and issued in 1893, with later editions to 1911. After the Library of Congress began publishing its own greatly expanded list of subject headings, the A.L.A. allowed its list to go out of print. Fortunately, the H.W. Wilson Company filled in the gap in 1923 with the publication of Minnie E. Sears' List of Subject Headings for Small Libraries. In addition to publications of the A.L.A., there are others issued by the various subdivisions of the organization. For example, the Association of College and Reference Libraries publishes a quarterly, College and Research Libraries. Other divisional publications include Public Libraries, the Journal of Cataloging and Classification, and Top of the News, with the latter being the official organ of the Division of Libraries for Children and Young People.

Several other important periodical and bibliographical aids for the librarian have been, and are, published by other companies. The Library Bureau of Remington Rand from 1896 to 1931 published a general library periodical entitled Public Libraries (later simply Libraries), which was edited by Mary Eileen Ahern. The University of Chicago Press has published the Library Quarterly since 1930, and also publishes a number of books in the library field, and F.W. Faxon Company issues various indexes, such as the Dramatic Index, begun in 1909, the Annual Magazine Subject Index (1907); Hanna Logasa's Index to One-Act Plays, and Mary Huse Eastman's Index to Fairy Tales. In 1952 another most useful library periodical was started by the University of Illinois Press, under the title of Library Trends.

Professional education

Before the twentieth century the librarian was for the most part a scholar, more concerned with learning than with the techniques of librarianship. His interest was in the contents of books, their subject matter, and he worked with books because he loved them. His interest in the use of books by others was secondary to his own use, or to his desire to preserve books for future use. Hence, even in the nineteenth century, the librarian was often considered to be a book-keeper, a protector of the storehouse of knowledge, rather than an educator, eager to have books used and read. Good librarians were apt to be so because they trained themselves or were fortunate enough to have worked under other great librarians. Library processes and methods varied from institution to institution, and usually each one developed its own method of arranging books and also of circulating them. Librarianship as a profession is virtually a twentieth century development.

Library education in England in the nineteenth century took the form of apprenticeships, and the prospective librarian simply learned his trade by working in a library. This method of library training was also preferred by many American libraries during the same period, and it was widely thought that apprenticeship was preferable to classroom training even as late as 1900. In Germany, on the other hand, the education of a librarian was the same as that of a scholar, and considerable emphasis was placed upon a wide range of knowledge in the liberal arts, considerable familiarity with languages, with the bibliography of all subjects, and even with rare books, and paleography. In America library education combined liberal education and training in the techniques and processes of library operation.

Some colleges had offered courses in bibliography, particularly historical bibliography, in the years immediately after the Civil War, and the University of Michigan began in 1881 to offer a course in reference and bibliography. In 1887 Melvil Dewey opened the first school of librarianship in the United States. Dewey's library school at Columbia endured for two years in the face of opposition. In 1889 he moved to Albany where he became Librarian of the New York State Library, and he carried his library school with him. He gradually built up a staff of teachers and a student body of thirty to fifty each year. His curriculum was a practical one. He taught the actual processes of selecting, acquiring, processing, arranging and circulating library books. His courses included phases of library work now considered clerical rather than professional, such as typewriting, library handwriting, book lettering, and book repairing.

Other institutions offered training in librarianship in the first decade after 1900. Schools offering library courses included Pratt, Drexel, Illinois, Syracuse, Carnegie of Pittsburgh, Simmons of Boston, Western Reserve of Cleveland, and the University of Wisconsin. In the public libraries, the training classes begun by Theresa Hitchler at the Astor Library became a full-time library school in the New York Public, and it was joined by similar courses at the Atlanta Carnegie Library, the St. Louis Public Library, the Los Angeles Public Library, and the California State Library at Sacramento. Both types of library training emphasized the practical aspects of librarianship, although the colleges usually required a liberal arts education as a prerequisite to admission to library science classes.

In 1913, the United States Bureau of Education reported on the status of library training in the nation, and noted the small number of colleges offering library training, or even training in the use of books and libraries. There was also considerable variance in the length and content of the courses given, and in the credit or degrees granted for library training.

Other colleges and universities in 1913 reported special summer courses for school or public librarians. The University of Wisconsin was most specific in describing its short course, which was not intended to graduate expert librarians. This summer course offered instruction in library handwriting, book selection, book buying methods, accessioning, shelf listing, classification, cataloging, bookplates, book labels, periodicals, reference books, book binding, preparation of reading lists, library furniture and traveling libraries. Of some 900 colleges and universities queried by the Bureau of Education, only ten per cent reported offering any training at all in the use of books and libraries.

The general view of library training prior to 1920 shows a most confused picture. There was no general conception of what should be taught in library science courses, or what education should be required. Different institutions admitted to their library courses high school graduates and university graduates. Also, library training was being offered by public libraries, technical schools, teachers colleges, liberal arts colleges, and universities, and there was no general agreement as to who was doing the best job. Some thought that any scholar could learn the necessary routines to run a library in short order, while others considered a sound training in the technique of operating a library more important than a knowledge of the contents of books. This confusion tended to work against the professional standing of the graduates of the various schools, so there soon arose a demand for standardization of library schools and their curricula. In 1915, ten library school joined together to form the Association of American Library Schools, with the purpose of standardizing entrance requirements and reforming curricula. This still did not solve the problems, however, and in 1919, Carnegie Corporation aid was obtained for a thorough study of the library training field. Charles C. Williamson, then on the New York Public Library staff, was employed to do the necessary research.

Williamson's report was completed and published in 1923, and in many respects it marks a turning point in the modern era of library training. Williamson surveyed the library school curricula, entrance requirements, teaching staffs, methods of instruction, and textbooks. He found confusion between professional and clerical training, and recommended that library schools teach professional work only, while training classes conducted by libraries should be used for teaching library techniques to clerical workers. He recommended more standardization in the library school curricula, particularly in the first year. He found only two library schools that required a college degree for admission, and he recommended that all should have this requirement. Concerning the teaching staffs in the library

188

schools, Williamson noted that only 52 percent were
college graduates themselves, only seven percent of
them had ever had any training in teaching, and nearly
a third had had little or no practical experience in library work. He particularly noted the lack of adequate
text-books, and the reliance on the lecture method of
teaching. He recommended better qualified teaching
personnel, more class discussion, more and better supervised field work, and improved textbooks. The need
for more library schools and more students was pointed
out, as well as the need for certification of professionally trained librarians. Finally, the necessity for post-
graduate library courses in specialized and advanced
fields was recognized, and considerable emphasis on
cultural rather than technical courses was encouraged.
On the whole, Williamson's findings concerning library
training were not flattering to the profession, but his
recommendations were sound, and, at least to some degree, they were gradually adopted over the next decade.

Along with the funds for Williamson's study, the Carnegie Corporation provided additional support for a ten
year period for the promotion and extension of library
training. A Board of Education for Librarianship was
established in 1924, and this group proceeded to plan
for the accreditation of library schools. It also aided
and encouraged the development of new library schools.
In 1926, the New York State Library School at Albany
was returned to Columbia University where it became
the School of Library Service. Dr. Williamson became
its head and was able to carry out some of his own
recommendations. The Carnegie Corporation also made
available funds for the establishment of two Southern
library schools, one at Hampton Institute, Virginia, for
Negroes, and one at the University of North Carolina.
It also aided in the establishment of the first graduate
school of library science, at the University of Chicago.
By 1929, graduate library courses, that is, courses beyond the first year, were offered at Michigan, Illinois,
California, Columbia and Chicago, and Carnegie fellow-
ships were available for the best qualified students ap-
plying for admissions at any of those schools. With the
beginning of advanced library study, leading to M.A. and
Ph.D. degrees in library science, the training of librarians entered a new phase.

By 1938, the Board of Education for Librarianship had accredited twenty-five library schools in the United States, with divisions into three classes to accomodate the differences between them. Type I schools required college graduation for admission and-or gave advanced library courses beyond the first year. Type II schools had the same entrance requirements, but gave only one year of library training. Type III schools admitted college undergraduates and gave only one year of library courses. In addition to these, however, there were a number of other colleges, particularly teacher training institutions, that offered courses in library science, usually for the training of school librarians.

Along with the idea of accreditation for library schools came the plea for certification of librarians, although this was somewhat slower to achieve general approval. By 1938, 21 states and the District of Columbia were legally requiring certification for school librarians, while a few states were beginning to certify public and county librarians, or librarians in state colleges and universities. By 1952, school librarians in 31 states were required to hold certificates, while only 14 states called for legal certification of public librarians. Standards for public libraries, were adopted by the American Library Association in 1933, and standards for junior colleges were drawn up by a Carnegie Corporation Advisory Group in 1937. State departments of education, and regional associations of colleges and secondary schools have set up standards for high school libraries, and the regional associations have also drawn up standards for college libraries. This combination of certification of librarians, and high standards for libraries has gone far toward improving libraries.

The Second World War brought on an increased demand for trained librarians, and to meet this demand many non-accredited library schools were begun, and various innovations were introduced into the curricula of the established library schools. This led to a period of confusion in the years after 1945, and to several attempts to straighten out this confusion. As early as 1926, most of the library schools had agreed to offer only an A.B. or B.S. in library science for the first year of graduate work, and to require two years for the

M.A. or M.S. in L.S. After the War, some schools began to offer the masters degree for the first year of graduate library courses to make the library degree equal to the fifth year M.A. available in most other fields. By 1952 the majority of the accredited library schools were giving the fifth year M.A.

In 1946, Joseph L. Wheeler, retired librarian of the Enoch Pratt Free Library in Baltimore, surveyed the field of library education again at the expense of the Carnegie Corporation, and reported on his findings. In his volume, Progress and Problems in Education for Librarianship, Wheeler noted that there was still much criticism of library schools for teaching too much detail, for being too elementary, too theoretical, and too slow in meeting the changing demands of the library profession. He found also that these criticisms were not wholly justified, and that the library schools were making headway in meeting all of them. However, he still felt that the library education picture was confused, and librarians themselves undecided as to what type of library training they wanted for their new assistants. Wheeler's recommendations included more strength and life for the Board of Education for Librarianship, and more standardization in methods, requirements and curricula for the schools. If necessary, fewer and better library schools would be preferable to more at lower standards. Yet he still called for a strong program for recruiting librarians, and better salaries and working conditions in order to make the field more attractive to young people. And strong throughout all his recommendations lay the thought that, above all, librarians should know and love books.

Other developments in library training in recent years have been brought on by the changing demands in the library field. To reach librarians already in service, summer workshops, special institutes and conferences are held at many institutions. More attention has been paid to pre-professional or non-professional education, and the well-educated librarian, at home in at least one other field besides library science, has become a common figure in library circles. In any event, the trend now seems to be toward librarians who are "educated" rather than "trained".

The professional associations

Closely associated with the growth of librarianship as a profession, and with the development of library schools, has been the development of the professional association. In the United States, the major library organization has been the American Library Association. From its hundred or so members at the beginning, it has grown steadily, reaching about 2000 members in 1920, and more than 20,000 by 1950. Very early in its history the organization saw the need of specialized subdivisions and in 1889 a College and Reference Library Section was formed, followed by a Trustees' Section in 1890. Later on, sections for Catalogers and Classifiers, Public Librarians, Junior College Librarians, Children's Librarians, and other special groups, committees and round tables were added as the need for them arose. Outside of A.L.A., but cooperating with it it many ways are such groups as the Music Library Association, the Theatre Library Association, the Special Libraries Association, the Association of American Library Schools, the Catholic Library Association, the Medical Library Association, and other special groups. In addition, the A.L.A. often cooperates with such related groups as the National Education Association, the Adult Education Association, the American Documentation Institute and the Bibliographical Society of America.

Besides its component divisions, the American Library Association also ties together a nationwide system of state, regional and local associations. Each of the states has a library association. These usually meet annually or biennially, and many of them have their own publications. Moreover, several parts of the United States have active regional library organizations, such as the Southeastern Library Association and the Southwestern Library Association. In many of the larger cities there are local library associations, of which some are largely social, but others are professionally active.

The objectives of the A.L.A. have not changed in general since its origin, but they have been enlarged and broadened as library service in the nation has increased. The first objectives of promoting library service for all Americans has still not been completely achieved, but great progress has been made so that today roughly 85 percent of the people of the United States are in reach of library service. Other objectives of raising library standards, improving library methods, increasing the number of trained librarians, assuring the professional status of librarianship, and providing helpful professional literature and library tools for working librarians, have all been more or less achieved, although most need continued attention. In recent years the A.L.A. has added to its objectives the obtaining of federal aid for libraries, and the promotion of international understanding through books and libraries.

Professionally, the American librarian has come far since 1876. He has achieved professional recognition, and a respected place in the educational structure of the country. There are still many problems concerning the recruitment and education of librarians, and concerning their duties, salaries and welfare after they are professionally trained, but these problems are gradually being solved. Today, the leaders of the profession recognize that both quantity and quality are needed among potential librarians, and that better librarians as well as more librarians are needed to serve a nation of intelligent readers.

Bibliography

American Library Association: In retrospect: a history of the Division of Cataloging and Classification. Chicago, 1950. 28 p.
------ The preparation of teacher-librarians. Chicago, 1937. 48 p.
Berelson, Bernard, ed.: Education for librarianship. Chicago, 1949. 307 p.
Beust, Nora E.: Professional library education. Washington, 1937. 95 p.
Bryan, Alice I.: The public librarian. New York, 1952. 474 p. (See especially pp. 299-451.)
Butler, Pierce: Introduction to library science. Chicago, 1933. 118 p.
Cutter, Charles A.: The expansive classification.
Dana, J.C.: The library primer. New York, 1920. 263 p. (1st ed. 1899).
Danton, J. Periam: Education for librarianship. New York, 1949. 97 p.

David, Lily M.: Economic status of library personnel, 1949. Chicago, 1950. 117 p.

Dewey, Melvil: Simplified library school rules. New York, 1904. 96 p.

Downs, Robert B.: Union catalogs in the U.S. Chicago, 1941 409 p.

Evans, Henry R: Library instruction in universities, colleges and normal schools. Washington, 1814. 38 p.

Feipel, Louis: Library binding manual. Chicago, 1951. 74 p.

Fleming, Edward M.: R.R. Bowker, militant liberal. Norman, Okla., 1952. 395 p.

Friedel, J.H.: Training for librarianship. Philadelphia, 1921. 224 p.

Joint Committee of the American Association of Teachers Colleges and the A.L.A.: How shall we educate teachers and librarians for library service in the school? New York, 1936, 74 p.

Lawler, John: The H.W. Wilson Company: half a century of bibliographical publishing. Minneapolis, 1950. 207 p.

Lehman-Haupt, Hellmut: The book in America. New York, 1939. 453 p.

Lyle, Guy R.: The administration of the college library. New York, 1949. 608 p.

Metcalf, Keyes D.: The program of instruction in library schools. Urbana, Ill., 1943. 49 p.

Miller, William: The book industry: a report of the Public Library Inquiry. New York, 1949. 156 p.

Munn, Ralph: Conditions and trends in education for librarianship. New York, 1936. 49 p.

Munthe, Wilhelm: American librarianship from a European angle. Chicago, 1939. 191 p.

Pettee, Julia: Subject headings: the history and theory of the alphabetical subject approach to books. New York, 1947. 191 p.

Plummer, Mary W.: Training for librarianship. Chicago, 1920. 24 p.

Reece, Ernest J.: Programs for library schools. New York, 1943. 64 p.

Rider, Fremont: Melvil Dewey. Chicago, 1944. 151 p.

Sawyer, H.P., ed.: The library and its contents. New York, 1925. 471 p.

Sawyer, Harriet P., ed.: The library as a vocation. New York, 1933. 484 p.

Tai, Tse-Chien: Professional education for librarianship. New York, 1925. 259 p.

Utley, George B.: 50 years of the American Library Association. Chicago, 1926. 29 p.

Wheeler, Joseph L.: Progress and problems in education for librarianship. New York, 1946. 97 p.

Wilson, H.W.: The bookman's reading and tools. New York, 1932. 53 p.

Williamson, Charles C.: Training for library service, a report prepared for the Carnegie Corporation of New York, 1923. 165 p.

Winchell, Constance M., ed.: Guide to reference books, 7th ed. Chicago, 1951. 645 p.

Graham, C.R.: "1876-1951, seventy five years later." Library Journal, LXXVI, (1951), 459.

Howe, Harriet E.: "Two decades in education for librarianship." Library Quarterly, XII, (1942), 557-570.

Keppel, F.P.: "The Carnegie Corporation and the graduate library school", Library Quarterly, I, (1931), 22-25.

Mitchell, Sydney B.: "The pioneer library school in middle age", Library Quarterly, XX (1950), 272-288.

"Philadelphia, 1876-1951," Library Journal, LXXVI, (1951), 1984-1986.

Putnam, Herbert: "Education for library work," Independent, LII, (November 22, 1900), 2773-2776.

Wilson, L.R.: "The American library school today", Library Quarterly, VII, (1937), 211-245.

Walbridge, E.F.: "Milestones of library history," Library Journal, LXXVI, (March 15, 1951), 460-463.

INDEX

Aberdeen, Scotland, University Library, 73, 149.
Academy of Natural Sciences Library, Philadelphia, 177.
Adams, James, 88, 97.
Adams, John, 105.
Adams, John Quincy, 119.
Advertising, 92.
Ahern, Mary Eileen, 185.
Albany Institute of Science Library, 112.
Alcuin, 30-31.
Alexandrian Library, 18-19.
Almanacs, 87, 89, 141.
Alphabet, 5, 7-9.
Alsted, Johann Heinrich, 69.
Ambrosian Library, Milan, 60, 153.
American Academy of Arts and Sciences Library, Boston, 112.
American Library Association, 130, 162, 168-170, 181, 183-185, 190, 192-193.
American Philosophical Society Library, Philadelphia, 112, 177.
American Red Cross, 162.
Amherst College Library, 110.
Amsterdam University Library, 67.
Antwerp, Belgium, Municipal Library, 67.
Appleton-Century-Crofts Company, 142.
Archives, 15, 16, 176.
Argentina, National Library, Buenos Aires, 148.
Argentina, National University Library, Buenos Aires, 148.
Aristides, 19.
Ascham, Roger, 74.
Association of American Library Schools, 188, 192.
Assurbanipal's library, 16-17.
Astor, John Jacob, 125.
Astor Library, New York City, 126, 161, 187.
Atlanta Carnegie Library, 187.
Auckland, New Zealand, Public Library, 157.
Audio-visual aids, 171-172.
Australia, National Library, Canberra, 156.
Austria, Royal Library, Vienna, 66.

Azilian pebbles, 3.
Balcarres, Earl of, 77.
Barnard, John, Jr., 100.
Baskerville, John, 81, 83.
Bates, Joshua, 125.
Bavarian State Library, Munich, 64, 151.
Bayle, Pierre, 69.
Behistun, Rock of, 7.
Belgium, Royal Library, Brussels, 67.
Benjamin Franklin Library, Mexico City, 147.
Bentley, Richard, 75.
Berkeley, George, 99.
Biblioteca Ambrosiana,
    See Ambrosian Library, Milan.
Biblioteca Casanatense, Rome, 153.
Biblioteca Lindesiana, Manchester, England, 77.
Bibliothèque Mazarine, Paris, 62-63, 150.
Bibliothèque Nationale, Paris, 62, 65, 76, 150.
Bibliothèque Ste. Genevieve, Paris, 63, 150.
Billings, John Shaw, 129, 161.
Bingham, Caleb, 115.
Bishop, William Warner, 153.
Blair, James, 99.
Blenham Castle Library, 77.
Block printing, 41-42, 44.
Board of Education for Librarianship, 189-191.
Bodleian Library,
    See Oxford University Library.
Bodley, Sir Thomas, 72, 79.
Bologna, Italy, University Library, 153.
Bonn, Germany, University Library, 151.
Book auctions, 106.
Book bindings, 28, 31, 32, 140-142.
Book collectors, 26-27,
    See also Libraries, Private.
Book forms, 11-12, 16, 20, 26, 48, 59, 140-141.
Book jackets, 140-141.
Book selection, 113, 181-182, 184-185.
Book trade, 17, 21-22, 34, 37-38, 58, 72, 106, 114, 141-143.
Boston Athenaeum, 123, 131, 179.
Boston Mercantile Library, 131.
Boston Public Library, 100, 104, 120, 123, 125, 130.
Boston Society of Natural History Library, 112.
Bowditch, Nathaniel, 125.

Bowdoin, James, 110.
Bowdoin College Library, 110.
Bowker, R.R., Company, 132, 181, 184.
Bradford, Andrew, 92-93.
Bradford, John, 97.
Bradford, William, 87, 93-94, 97.
Braud, Denis, 97.
Bray, Thomas, 78, 101.
Brazil, National Library, Rio de Janeiro, 147.
Breslau, Germany, University Library, 151.
Bristol, England, Public Library, 78.
British Library Association, 149.
British Museum Library, 74-77, 80, 149, 150.
Broadsides, 69, 90.
Brown, John, 110.
Brown University Library, 100, 109, 124.
Budapest University Library, 156.
Budé, Guillaume, 62.
Buell, Abel, 93.
Byrd, William, 104-105.
Caesar, Julius, 19.
Caldwell, Joseph, 110.
California State Library, Sacramento, 187.
California, University of, 189.
Callimachus, 18.
Cambridge University Library, 72-74, 77, 80, 149.
Camden, William, 77.
Campbell, John, 91.
Carnegie, Andrew, 133, 161.
Carnegie Corporation, 153, 170, 188-191.
Carnegie Institute Library School, 187.
Caslon, William, 81, 83.
Cassiodorus, 27.
Catalogs and cataloging, 16, 18, 23, 28, 35, 59, 62, 65,
    100, 124, 125, 128-129, 131-132, 148-149, 166, 181,
    184.
Cave drawings, 2.
Caxton, William, 50, 51, 53, 80, 82.
Cennini, Bernardo di, 51.
Censorship, 89-90, 94, 151-152.
Certification of librarians, 170, 189-190.
Chained books, 28, 34.
Chambers, Ephraim, 69, 83.
Champollion, Jean François, 6.
Chap-books, 58.

Charlemagne, 30-31.
Charleston, S.C., Library Society, 102.
Chicago Public Library, 162.
Chicago, University of, 189.
Children's literature, 82, 141-142.
Chile, National Library, Santiago, 148.
Chile, University of, Santiago, 148.
China, National Library, Peking, 158.
Church, William, 137.
Cincinnati Public Library, 120, 162.
Classification, 30, 63, 111, 113, 124, 132, 181. See
    also Library arrangement.
Clay tablets, 6-7, 16-17.
Clog almanac, 3.
Clymer, George, 136.
Codex, 12.
Cogswell, Joseph G., 126.
Columbia University Library, 100, 109.
Columbia University School of Library Service, 131,
    186, 189.
Columbian press, 136.
Colwell, Stephen, 120.
Copenhagen University Library, 67.
Copperplate engraving, 72, 139.
Copyright, 79-80, 120.
Cotton, Robert Bruce, 75.
Coventry, England, Public Library, 78.
Cracow, Poland, University Library, 68.
Crantz, Martin, 51.
Cremer, Heinrich, 45.
Cronberger, Juan, 86.
Cuba, National Library, Havana, 149.
Cuneiform writing, 7.
Cutter, Charles A., 131, 132.
David Ibn Nachmias, 52.
Davie, William R., 110.
Davis, James, 88, 97.
Day, Matthew, 86-87, 97.
Day, Stephen, 86-87.
DeBury, Richard, 35.
Demotic writing, 6.
Denmark, Royal Library, Copenhagen, 67, 154.
Dewey, Melvil, 130-132, 180, 186.
Diamond Sutra, 41.
Dickinson College Library, 110.

199

Diderot, Denis, 69.
Drexel Institute Library School, 131, 187.
Duke's Library, Wolfenbüttel, Germany, 64, 66.
Dummer, Jeremiah, 99.
Dundee, Scotland, Public Library, 78.
Du Pont Company libraries, 178.
Dürer, Albrecht, 59.
Durham, England, University Library, 74.
Dury, John, 74.
Eastman, Mary Huse, 185.
Ebert, Fritz, 66.
Edinburgh University Library, 73, 77, 149.
Electrotype, 137.
Elieser, Rabbi, 52.
Elzevir Press, Leiden, 49.
Enoch Pratt Free Library, Baltimore, 132, 191.
Encyclopedias, 69, 83, 141, 143.
Essex Institute Library, Salem, Mass., 129.
Estienne, Henri, 49-50.
Everett, Edward, 125.
Exchanges, 121.
Faxon, F.W., Company, 185.
Federal aid to libraries, 175, 193.
Fitzwilliam, Lord, 77.
Folger Shakespeare Library, Washington, D.C., 176.
Force, Peter, 120.
Foster, John, 97.
Fourdrinier brothers, 138.
Fowle, Daniel, 97.
France, National Assembly Library, Paris, 150.
France, National Library,
  See Bibliothèque Nationale.
Franklin, Ann, 94.
Franklin, Benjamin, 88-89, 93, 97, 101.
Franklin, James, 97.
Franklin Institute Library, Philadelphia, 112.
Freedom of the press, 90, 95.
  See also Censorship.
Freiburg, Germany, University Library, 151.
French Institute Library, Paris, 150.
Friburger, Michael, 51.
Friends of the Library groups, 167.
Froben, Johann, 49.
Fust, Johann, 45, 51.
Garamond, Claude, 50.

Mentelin, Johann, 51.
Meredith, Hugh, 88.
Mergenthaler, Othmar, 138.
Mexico, National Library, Mexico City, 146-147.
Michigan, University of, 186, 189.
Microphotography, 167.
Minsk, Russia, State Library, 155.
Mitchell, William H., 137.
Mnemonic devices, 3-4.
Moreri, Louis, 69.
Morrill Act of 1862, 126.
Moscow Public Library, 68.
Moscow University Library, 68.
Moseley, Edward, 105.
Mudge, Isadore G., 185.
Mussey, W.H., 120.
Nairne, James, 77.
Naples University Library, 153.
National Central Library, Florence, Italy, 153.
National Council of Teachers of English, 169-170.
National Education Association, 168-170, 192.
National Youth Administration, 167.
Naudé, Gabriel, 62-64.
Netherlands Royal Library, 67.
New Hampshire Library Act, 123.
New Hampshire State Library, 119.
New South Wales State Library, Sydney, 157.
New York Academy of Medicine Library, 177.
New York Academy of Sciences Library, 112.
New York Apprentices' Library, 114.
New York City Hospital Library, 129.
New York Engineering Societies Library, 177.
New York Historical Society Library, 129.
New York Mercantile Library, 124.
New York Public Library, 125-126, 132, 161-162.
New York Society Library, 102.
New York State Library, 119, 186, 189.
New York Times Library, 177.
New Zealand National Library Service, 157.
Newberry, Walter L., 133.
Newberry Reference Library, Chicago, 133, 176.
Newbery, John, 82.
Newspapers, 69, 88, 91-92, 141.
Newton, Sir Isaac, 99.
North Carolina University Library, 110, 189.

Plantin family, 49, 51.
Playing cards, 42, 44.
Plutarch, 17.
Poland, National Library, Warsaw, 156.
Pollio, Caius Asinius, 19.
Poole, William Frederick, 131, 162.
Portugal, National Library, Lisbon, 68.
Pratt, Enoch, 132.
Pratt Institute Library School, 131, 187.
Prince, Thomas, 104, 125.
Princeton University Library, 100, 109, 165.
Printing, 41-55, 58-60, 80, 86-97, 136-144.
Propaganda, 152, 154-156, 158.
Prussian State Library, Berlin, 63-64.
Public Relations, 172.
Putnam, Herbert, 132.
Pynson, Richard, 52-53.
Quipus, 3.
Radio, 143.
Ranganathan, S. R., 158.
Rawlinson, Sir Henry, 7.
Redwood, Abraham, 104.
Redwood Library, Newport, R.I., 102, 104.
Ricardo, Antonio, 86.
Riessinger, Sixtus, 51.
Rind, William, 106.
Rittenhouse, William, 93.
Rolls, 11-12, 16, 20, 32.
Rood, Theodoric, 52.
Rosenwald Fund, 170.
Rosetta Stone, 6.
Rotary Press, 136.
Roulstone, George, 97.
Royal Society Library, London, 77.
Roycroft, Thomas, 81.
Russia, Imperial Library, St. Petersburg, 68, 154.
Rutledge, John, 105.
St. Andrews University Library, 73.
St. Louis Public Library, 187.
St. Mark's Library, Venice, 60.
St. Petersburg, Russia, Academy Library, 68.
Sammonicus, 21.
San Marco, Italy, Library, 36, 37.
San Marcos National University Library, Lima, 148.
Sauer, Christopher, 93, 97.

Tory, Geoffrey, 52.
Trinity College, Dublin, Library, 73-74.
Trow, John F., 137.
Troyes, France, Municipal Library, 63.
Type-casting machines, 137.
Type-founding, 49-50, 93.
Type-setting machine, 137, 138.
Typography, 81.
  See also Printing.
Ulpian Library, Rome, 20.
Union catalogs, 167.
UNESCO, 159.
U.S. Armed Forces Medical Library, 174.
U.S. Army Artillery School Library, 118-119.
U.S. Army Bureau of Ordnance Library, 118.
U.S. Atomic Energy Commission libraries, 174.
U.S. Department of Agriculture Library, 129, 173-174.
U.S. Department of Defense libraries, 174.
U.S. Department of Interior Library, 129.
U.S. Government Printing Office, 142.
U.S. Information Service libraries, 175.
U.S. Library of Congress, 117-118, 120, 121, 123, 127-
  129, 173-174, 181, 184-185.
U.S. Military Academy Library, 118, 174.
U.S. Navy Department, Library Services Branch, 174.
U.S. Office of Education Library, 129, 169, 175, 187.
U.S. Patent Office Library, 119.
U.S. President's Advisory Committee on Education, 175.
U.S. State Department Library, 118, 121.
U.S. Surgeon General's Library, 129.
U.S. Treasury Department Library, 118.
U.S. War Department Library, 118.
Uppsala University Library, 67.
Urbino, Italy, Library, 36, 61.
Usher, James, 74.
Utrecht, Netherlands, University Library, 67.
Vatican Library, Rome, 36-37, 61, 153.
Vellum, 11, 43.
Venezuela, National Library, Caracas, 148.
Vespasiano de Bisticci, 36.
Virginia University Library, 111.
Victor Emanuel National Library, Rome, 153.
Victoria State Library, Melbourne, 157.
Victoria University Library, Manchester, England, 74.
Vienna University Library, 67.

Waldfogel, Procopius, 46.
Wampum, 3.
War damage to libraries, 150, 152, 155, 157.
Warsaw University Library, 156.
Washington, George, 105.
Watterson, George, 118.
Waxed tablets, 11-12.
Webb, George, 97.
Western Reserve University Library School, 187.
Wheeler, Joseph L., 191.
William and Mary College Library, 98-99.
Williamson, Charles C., 188-189.
Wells, William C., 97.
Wilson, H.W., Company, 143, 180, 182-185.
Whittington, Richard, 35.
Winchell, Constance M., 185.
Winsor, Justin, 130.
Wisconsin State Historical Society Library, 129, 177.
Wisconsin University Library School, 187.
Wood cuts, 48-49, 59, 83, 139.
    See also Block books.
Works Progress Administration library program, 163,
    167.
Writing, 1-12, 30.
Writing materials, 5, 6, 9, 10-12.
Wynkyn de Worde, 52, 53.
Yale, Elihu, 99.
Yale University Library, 99, 109, 111, 123, 124, 165,
    168.
Zainer, Gunther, 51.
Zarotti, Antonio, 51.
Zell, Ulrich, 51.
Zenger, Peter, 90.

Coll.